Python Coding

Tools and Basics for Beginners

Travis Booth

Books by Travis Booth

Scan the Code to Learn More

Machine Learning Series

Machine Learning With Python: Hands-On Learning for Beginners

Machine Learning With Python: An In Depth Guide Beyond the Basics

Python Data Analytics Series

Python Data Analytics: The Beginner's Real World Crash Course

Python Data Analytics: A Hands-On Guide Beyond the Basics

Python Data Science Series

Python Data Science: Hands-On Learning for Beginners

Python Data Science: A Hands-On Guide Beyond the Basics

Deep Learning Series

Deep Learning With Python: A Hands-On Guide for Beginners

Deep Learning With Python: A Comprehensive Guide Beyond the Basics

Bonus Offer: Get the Ebook absolutely free when you purchase the paperback via Kindle Matchbook!

Contents

Introduction... - 1 -

Chapter 1: Python - Features and Setup............................- 5 -

    Python Setup on Windows...- 7 -

    Verifying your Python Installation.. - 8 -

    Python – Basic Syntax.. - 9 -

    First Python Program... - 9 -

    Python Identifiers...- 9 -

Chapter 2: Basic Operators of Python Language....................... - 11 -

    Types of Operators..- 11 -

    Python Arithmetic Operators.. - 11 -

    Python Comparison Operators...- 13 -

    Python Assignment Operators.. - 16 -

    Python Bitwise Operators.. - 17 -

    Python Logical Operator.. - 19 -

    Python Membership Operator..- 20 -

    Python Identity Operators... - 22 -

    Python Operator Precedence... - 24 -

Chapter 3: Basic Variable Types...- 26 -

    Numbers..- 26 -

    String..- 28 -

    Single-Quoted Strings...- 29 -

    The str and repr in Strings.. - 30 -

    String Methods... - 33 -

    String Format..- 35 -

Raw Strings, Long Strings & Unicode..- 37 -

Dictionaries in Python...- 39 -

Reading Input and Printing...- 44 -

Chapter 4: Logical Thinking & Data Sets...................................- 46 -

Python Data Types...- 46 -

Python Sets...- 50 -

How to Access Items in a Set...- 51 -

Checking Different Values in a Set...- 52 -

Adding Single and Multiple Items to Sets................................- 53 -

Finding the Length of Sets...- 54 -

How to Remove Items from the Sets..- 55 -

The Discard Method...- 56 -

The Pop() Method..- 57 -

How to Clear a Set of Values...- 59 -

How to Update a Set with New Values.....................................- 59 -

Deleting a Set...- 59 -

Chapter 5: Introduction to Loops...- 66 -

Types of Loops..- 68 -

While Loop..- 69 -

Infinite Loops..- 71 -

For Loops..- 72 -

The Range Function...- 73 -

Iterating by Sequence Index..- 77 -

Nested Loops..- 78 -

Break..- 79 -

Continue Statement.. - 82 -

Pass Statement..- 83 -

Using Else Statement with Loops... - 84 -

Chapter 6: Python Lists & Tuples.. - 86 -

Examples.. - 86 -

How to Access the Elements.. - 87 -

Operations in List.. - 88 -

List Slices.. - 88 -

Mutable Lists... - 89 -

List Deletion..- 90 -

Tuples Introduction... - 90 -

Tuple Packing.. - 91 -

Nested Tuple.. - 93 -

Access Values in Tuple..- 93 -

Updating a Tuple... - 96 -

Deleting Tuple...- 97 -

Type of Operator..- 97 -

Types of Methods.. - 98 -

Advantages of Tuple..- 100 -

Chapter 7: Python Exception Handling...................................- 101 -

Assertions in Python... - 101 -

What is an Exception?... - 101 -

Handling an Exception.. - 102 -

Exception Clause with No Exception..................................... - 103 -

Exception Clause with Multiple Exception........................... - 103 -

The Try-Finally Clause.. - 104 -

Arguments in Exception... - 105 -

Raising an Exception... - 105 -

User-Defined Exception.. - 106 -

Chapter 8: The If Statements... - 107 -

How to Define a Function... - 112 -

How to Pass Information to a Function................................ - 113 -

A Look at Function Arguments and Parameters.................. - 115 -

How to Pass a List to the Function as a Parameter............. - 117 -

Positional Arguments... - 121 -

Keyword Arguments... - 125 -

A Look at Argumentative Errors in Functions.................... - 126 -

Python Arrays... - 128 -

Loop the Elements of an Array.. - 130 -

Chapter 9: Python Classes... - 134 -

Creating an Instance from the Cat Class............................ - 138 -

How to Call the Methods... - 140 -

How to Work with Classes and Instances in Python.......... - 145 -

How to Modify the Value of an Attribute by a Dedicated Method..... - 151 -

Child Class and Parent Class... - 157 -

Chapter 10: File Navigation with Python............................ - 160 -

Reading Information from a File.. - 160 -

Pattern Matching... - 162 -

Exploring the Match Object... - 165 -

Conclusion.. - 167 -

Introduction

Programming is not an easy thing to do. Perhaps you've tried it before and are intimidated. Or if you're going to be like most readers of this book, you have some programming experience and are looknig to get your hands dirty with Python. It seems to be everywhere these days.

So, what is Python, and what makes it different from other programming languages? Why is everyone crazy about learning and using Python? According to its official website www.python.org, Python is considered an object-oriented, well-interpreted and a very high-level programming language that has dynamic semantics. They have condensed the real meaning of Python into a few words. Most of the terms used in this definition will stand transparent and clear as you progress through this book.

In short, Python is a smart language and facilitates programmers when they are creating a program. It helps you to get the level of functionality that is required during the creation of a program. It knows how to stay out of your way and how to save you from undue hassles while you are consuming your energy on composing lengthy codes. You will be able to write programs that are readable, clear and comprehendible. In short, Python has a lot more to offer than most of the other programming languages out there in the market.

Tibay sometimes disagrees with me, saying that Python is not as fast as C or C++. But it is not always about the speed. It is also about the ease of use and comprehension of code, in addition to understanding the errors you commit during composing codes. Tibay adds that you can save a great deal of time during the course of programming, which many other programming languages don't offer. The difference in the speed is remarkable. Even if you don't know the basics of programming, Python is so easy that you can start using this language right away.

A Brief History of Python

Python was conceived by Guido Van Rossum during the 1980s. Guido was a member of the National Research Institute of Mathematics and Computer Science. Python was initially created as a response to the ABC programming language. But it surpassingly introduced exception handling. In general, it was targeted at the Amoeba OS.

While most people think that Python is named after the killing machine, the Python snake, you will be intrigued to know that Python is named after the British show Monty Python. You can find lots of versions of Python on the internet. This makes Python quite similar to other programming languages, which also go through lots of versions before reaching the final stage of maturity. Apart from exception handling, you can find ordinary features like lists, classes, and strings in Python. In addition, you can also make use of filter, lambda, and reduce in Python. These features have empowered Python for functional programming.

In 2002 we witnessed the release of Python 2.0. This version was like an open source project. There were list comprehensions and a garbage collector. In late 2008, Python 3 was released. This was the next as well as the latest version of Python.

The evolution of Python 3 has since started and it runs flawlessly and endlessly. Although Python 3 has been introduced, most programmers are using Python 2 to create programs.

Who is this book for?

The basic objective behind writing this book is to educate you about Python basics and some advanced methods of programming and automation. You will learn to create programs that actually work. This book will give you a solid foundation on which you can stand and from which you can take a flight towards the advanced level of Python programming, such as creating your own games and automating different things. This book is for those who have not yet entered into the realm of programming. After learning the basics of Python, you can go on to learn interesting things with a clear mind. If you want to learn the basics of Python programming and solve problems related to your own computer, this book is definitely for you. Read the entire book become acquainted with some real coding. Students, teachers, and business owners can all benefit from learning Python.

Pre-Requisites for this Book

Well, there are no hard and fast rules for this section. You can start from anywhere, but it is recommended that you that intuitive right from the start. You should have a working computer in your home or a laptop with an operating system installed on it. The first step is to install Python by downloading it from their official website. Once it is installed, you are perfectly ready for reading the book. You need to install Python because you will have to run code snippets which I have created for you in the book. You can be a person who doesn't even have a working knowledge of Python programming. So, just relax and focus on the steps that are given in the book for mastering the art of Python programming. I don't guarantee that after a single read you will be a master of Python. What I can assure you is that you will be able to move on to higher positions in the world of Python coding.

What this Book has to Offer

This book will help you become a Python programmer at a beginners' level. When you have walked through the book, you will be able to comprehend the language of coding very well, and you will be able to grasp more in-depth knowledge on the subject. The book is divided into sections named as chapters. Let's see what it has to offer to the readers.

The first chapter contains the basics of Python. It lets you know how to install Python shell on your computer system, the basic syntax of Python, and identifiers.

The second chapter covers Python operators, including arithmetic operators, logical operators, assignment operators, bitwise operators, identity operators, comparison operators, and membership operators.

The third chapter discusses variables. How can you assign a value to a variable? It goes on to discuss different kinds of variables like strings and numbers. Then the chapter turns toward highlighting the importance and usage of dictionaries. It introduces methods to create a dictionary, and ways to use the dictionaries.

The fourth chapter sheds light on logical thinking and data sets. It contains useful information on the if-statements.

The next chapter is centered around Python loops. I will be discussing the while loop and the for loop in addition to talking about the range function.

This brings us to the sixth chapter which is about Python lists and tuples. You will learn how to create a list and access the elements present in the list. In addition to this, you will be able to create tuples.

The seventh chapter is about exception handling in Python.

Now that you have reached the eighth chapter, it is time to go through the if-statements which are necessary if you want your machine to make a decision on the basis of logical reasoning.

The ninth is about Python classes. You can create real objects which act on your direction. You will learn to create your own classes and instances for modeling objects on real life things.

The last chapter of the book is about navigating files in the Python system and pattern matching.

Chapter 1: Python - Features and Setup

Python is an Object-oriented language that was authored by Guido van Rossum. It is a high-level, object-oriented language, that is powerful for programming. It is used in a vast array of domains including web application development, database access, desktop GUI's, and scientific & numeric computing. Let's see some of the common applications of Python.

Python is well-known because of its use as a general-purpose language. There are lots of areas where Python can be used for development purposes. Let's take a look at some of them.

Web Applications

Python is widely used for the development of a number of web applications. There are Python libraries that can handle XML and HTML, Feedparser and email systems. Python also has the ability to design different web applications by offering different frameworks like Flask as well as Django.

Desktop GUI Apps

Python provides libraries for development of user interface in Python based apps.

In addition to this it also helps in the development of certain software.

Some of the key features of Python are:

- Ease and Simplicity: Python has an elegant syntax, making the programs easier to write and maintain
- Language of Choice: the ease of use makes it a perfect candidate for prototyping development and ad-hoc programming.

- Runs Anywhere: Python supports a wide array of operating systems, including MacOS X, Windows, Linux, and Unix.
- Free software: Python is free for use and can also be freely modified and re-distributed. It is supported by a wide community of open source contributors.
- Object oriented: Python is an object-oriented language with support for classes and multiple inheritance.
- Significant whitespace: Python uses significant whitespaces instead of the curly braces/begin-end block for delimiting blocks.
- REPL: REPL is the python language shell which is short-form for Read, Eval, Print and Loop. The python shell, reads user input, evaluates, prints the results and loops back to the shell.
- Exceptions: Python has support for throwing and handling exceptions, resulting in cleaner error handling.
- Standard Library: Python comes with a great standard library which forms the crux of a huge universe. The standard library supports a wide variety of common programming tasks, such as file i/o, web programming, text search etc.
- Memory Manager: Python's memory manager handles the memory allocations and various dynamic memory management aspects freeing the user to focus on programming logic rather than complex allocations/deallocations of memory.

Some of the key third-party libraries that support the python standard library in the different domains are:

- Web frameworks: Django, flask, pyramid
- Data Science:Astropy, biopython, numpy,
- Cloud configuration – Ansible, Boto3 for AWS
- Data analytics – Pandas, Bokeh, TensorFlow

Python Setup on Windows

- Visit the official <u>python</u> website
- Navigate via the downloads tab to the downloads for windows

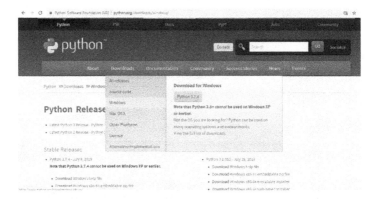

- Click the button to begin downloading the latest python 3 version
- Click on the downloaded file and select "Run the installer"
- After the installer starts, ensure that the "Add python to PATH" option is selected.

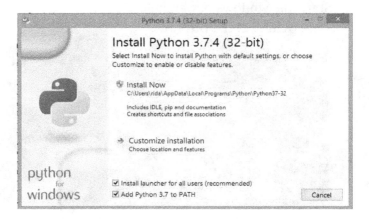

- Click on "Install Now"

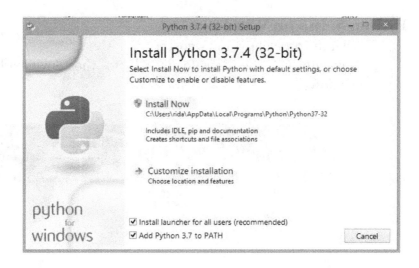

You may be warned to allow the python installer to make changes to your computer, which you should accept.
After a few minutes, the installer will complete, after which you should close the installer.

Verifying your Python Installation
- Start the windows powershell
- Type python at the prompt

- You will be taken to the "Triple arrow point" which indicates that python is waiting for your input.
- Welcome to Python!!

Python – Basic Syntax

Python is quite similar to other programming languages like Java, C++, and C# when it comes to basic syntax. Let us see the basic syntax in detail.

First Python Program

In order to execute your first "Hello World" program in Python, you need to enter the below statement in the prompt and then press the Enter key.

```
>>> print ("Hello World")
```

This will print Hello World on the screen.

Python Identifiers

Identifier is the name that we use for identifying the different variables, classes, methods, objects, etc. in a program. Each identifier name has to be unique and can't be used twice in the program for declaration of variables, classes, or methods.

The basic rules to create an identifier are:

1. It should start with small case a to z or capital case A to Z, or with underscore sign (_). After assigning the first letter, you can use digits as well from 0 to 9.
2. Special characters like $, @, % are not allowed to be used in the identifiers.
3. Identifier is case sensitive. Therefore, identifier name **Salary** and **salary** are considered as two different ones in Python programming language.
4. You can't use a reserved word as an identifier in Python, such as break, class, while, lambda, for, from, print, raise, etc.

Now let us see some naming conventions while creating identifiers in Python.

1. All Class names will start with A-Z. Remaining identifiers can be written as a-z. For example: Employee, Students, Hospital.
2. If the identifier starts with a single underscore, it means that it is a private identifier.
3. If the identifier starts with a double underscore, it means that it is a strong private identifier.
4. If the identifier ends with double underscore, it means that it is a language specific identifier name.

Chapter 2: Basic Operators of Python Language

Python is considered a high-level programming language with less complexity when it comes to using the basic operators in the code. It is built to read and implement computer language with ease. Python provides various types of operators for performing tasks. Let us see the basic operators provided by Python.

Types of Operators

1. Python Arithmetic Operators
2. Python Assignment Operators
3. Python Comparison Operators
4. Python Logical Operators
5. Python Bitwise Operators
6. Python Membership Operators
7. Python Identity Operators

Python Arithmetic Operators

Arithmetic operators help us to do several types of mathematical problems like addition, subtraction, multiplication, exponential values, floor divisions, etc.

Let's suppose we have two variables whose values are x = 16, y = 4.

Operator	Description of the operator	Example
Addition (+)	This operator will be adding the values on both sides of operands.	x + y = 20

Subtraction (-)	This operator will be subtracting the right-hand side value from the left-hand side value of the operand.	$x - y = 12$
Multiplication (*)	This operator will be multiplying the two values on both sides of the operands.	$x * y = 64$
Division (/)	This operator will be dividing the left-hand side value by the right-hand side value of the operand.	$x / y = 4$
Modulus (%)	This operator will be dividing the left-hand side value by the right hand side value of the operand and returns the left over remainder.	$x \% y = 0$
Exponent (**)	This operator will be doing the 'exponential power' calculation on operands.	$x ** y = 16$ to the power 4
Floor division (//)	This operator will be dividing the operands, the quotient of a number which is divided by 2 is the result.	$13 // 3 = 4$, simultaneously $13.0 // 3.0 = 4.0$;

Example: Let's see how the output comes {* values in [ ] are the outputs}

Suppose three variables are there having the values x = 25, y = 30, z = 0:

```
#!/usr/bin/python3
z = x + y
print(" result of z is ", z)
z = x - y
print(" result of z is ", z)
z = x * y
print(" result of z is ", z)
z = x / y
print(" result of z is ", z)
z = x % y
print(" result of z is ", z)
```

Output: [z = 35], [z = -5], [z = 750], [z = 0.833], [z = 5] respectively.

Now suppose,
a = 4, b = 5, c = a**b;
print("value of c is", c)
a = 15, b = 45, c = a//b;
print("value of c is", c)

Outputs: [c = 4 to the power 5 i.e. 1024;], [c = 3, as the quotient of 45/15 is 3;] respectively.

Python Comparison Operators

In python, comparison operators are operators that compare two operands' values and returns true or false in case of whether the condition has matched or not. It is also called Python Relational Operator.

Let's take two variables having the values a = 20, b = 15;

Operat or	Description of the operator	Example

(==)	This condition becomes true only if two given values (operands) are equal.	(a == b) → not true
(!=)	This condition becomes true only if the two operands aren't equal.	(a != b) → true
(>)	This condition becomes true only if the left operand is greater than the right operand.	(a > b) → true
(<)	This condition becomes true only if the right operand is greater than the left operand.	(a < b) → not true
(>=)	This condition becomes true only if the left operand is greater than or equal to the right operator.	(a >= b) → true
(<=)	This condition become true only if the right operand is greater than or equal to the left operand.	(a <= b) → not true

Example: Let's see how the output comes. {values in [ ] are outputs}

```
#!/usr/bin/python3
i = 10
j = 15
if ( i ==j )
    print("i is equal to j")
else
    print("i is not equal to j")
if ( i != i)
    print("i is not equal to j")
else
    print("i is equal to j")
if ( i > j)
    print("i is greater than j")
else
    print("i is not greater than j")
if ( i < j)
    print("i is less than j")
else
    print("i is not less than j")
if ( i >= j)
    print("i is greater than or equal to j")
else
    print("i is neither greater than nor equal to j")
if ( i <= j)
    print ("i is less than or equal to j")
else
    print("i is neither less than nor equal to j")
```

Outputs of the recently used comparison operators.

i is not equal to j
i is not equal to j
i is not greater than j
i is less than j
i is neither greater than nor equal to j
i is less than or equal to j

Python Assignment Operators

These kinds of operators are used to assign several values to the variables. Let's check the different types of assignment operators.

Operator	Description of the operator	Example
Equal (=)	This operator will assign values from right side operand to left side operand.	c = a + b;
Add AND (+=)	This operator will add the right operand with left operand and assigns the sum to left operand.	c += a → it is equivalent to c = c + a;
Subtract AND (-=)	This operator will subtract the right operand from left operand and assigns the subtraction to left operand.	c -= a → it is equivalent to c = c - a;
Multiply AND (*=)	This operator will multiply the right and left operand and assigns the multiplication to left operand.	c *= a → it is equivalent to c = c * a;
Divide AND (/=)	This operator will divide the left operand with right operand and assigns division to left operand.	c /= a → it's equivalent to c = c/a;
Modulus AND (%=)	This operator takes modulus by using both sides' operand and assigns the outcome to left operand.	c %= a → it's equivalent to c = c % a;
Exponent AND (**=)	Does 'to the power' calculation and assigns the outcome to the left operand.	c **= a → it's equivalent to c = c**a

Floor division AND (//=)	It does floor division and assigns the outcome to the left operand.	c //= a → it's equivalent to c = c // a;

Let's see the example.

```
#!/usr/bin/python3
a = 15
b = 20
c = 0

c = a + b
print("value of c is", c)

c += a
print("value of c is", c)

c *= a
print("value of c is", c)

c %= a
print("value of c is", c)
```

Output: 35, 50, 525, 5 are the outputs of the operators respectively.

Python Bitwise Operators

Bitwise operators are used to perform bit operations. All the decimal values will be converted in the binary format here.
Let us suppose:
a = 0101 1010
b = 0001 1000

(a & b) = 0001 1000
(a | b) = 0101 1010
(a ^ b) = 0100 0010
(~a)   = 1010 0101

Note: There is an in-built function [bin ()] in python that can obtain binary representation of an integer number.

Types of Bitwise Operators: [a = 0001 1000, b = 0101 1010]

Operators	Description of the operator	Example
Binary AND (&)	This operator executes a bit if it exists in both operands.	(a & b) is 0001 1000
Binary OR (|)	This operator executes a bit if it exists in one of the operands.	(a | b) is 0101 1010
Binary XOR (^)	This operator executes a bit if it is fixed in one operand but not in both	(a ^ b) is 0100 0010
Binary one's complement (~)	This operator executes just by flipping the bits.	~a = 1110 ~b = 0110
Binary left shift (<<)	This operator executes by moving left operand's value more left. It's specified by the right operand.	a << 100 (means 0110 0000)
Binary right shift (>>)	This operator executes by moving left operand's value right. It's specified by the right operand.	a >> 134 (means 0000 0110)

Let's see an example.

```
#!/usr/bin/python3

a = 50            # 50 = 0011 0010
b = 17            # 17 = 0001 0001

print('a=', a, ':', bin(a), 'b=', b, ':', bin(b))


c = 0
c = a & b;        # 16 = 0001 0000

print("result of AND is", c, ':', bin(c))


c = a | b;      # 51 = 0011 0011
print("result of OR is", c, ':', bin(c))


c = a ^ b;      # 66 = 0100 0010
print("result of XOR is", c, ':', bin(c))


c = a>> 2;      # 96 = 0110 0000
print("result of right shift is", c, ':', bin(c))
```

Output:
Result of AND is 16 → 0b010000
Result of OR is 51 → 0b110011
Result of XOR is 66 → 0b01000010
Result of right shift is 96 → 0b01100000

Python Logical Operator

Logical operator permits a program to make decisions according to multiple conditions. Every operand is assumed as a condition that can give us a true or false value. There are 3 types of logical operators.

(a = false operand, b = true operand.)

Operators	Description of the operator	Example
Logical And(AND)	If the given operands both are true, the condition becomes true	Condition is false.
Logical or(OR)	If one of the given operands is true, the condition becomes true.	Condition is true.
Logical not(NOT)	If the given operand is true, the condition becomes false.	Condition is true (for a) and false(for b).

Example:

```
>>> i = 25
# Logical AND Example
>>> if i < 30 AND i > 18:
        print (" Condition is fulfilled ")
else:
        print(" Condition is not fulfilled ")

# Logical OR Example
>>> if i < 18 OR i > 20:
        print(" Condition is fulfilled ")
else:
        print(" Condition is not fulfilled ")
```

Output:
Condition is fulfilled
Condition is fulfilled

Python Membership Operator

Membership operators are operators that validate the membership of a value. It examines for membership in a sequence like strings, list, tuples, etc. Two types of membership operators are:

Opera tor	Description of Operator	Example
In	The condition becomes true if it can find a variable in a specified sequence.	Follow the example part given below.
not in	The condition becomes true if it can find no variable in a specified sequence.	Follow the example part given below.

Example:

```
#!/usr/bin/python3

i = 40, j = 20;

listValues = {10, 20, 30, 40}

if( i is in the listValues )

print(" i is available in the list ")

else

print(" i is not available in the list ")

if(j is in the listValues)

print(" j is available in the list ")

else

print(" j is not available in the list ")

k = i / j
```

```
if( k is in the listValues)

print (" k is available in the list ")

else

print(" k is not available in the list ")
```

Output:

i is no available in the list.

j is not available in the list.

k is available in the list.

Python Identity Operators

These are operators that are used to determine whether a value is of a particular class or type. To determine the type of data which contains a number of variables, this type of operator is used. There are two types of Identity operators as shown below:

Operator	Description of the operator	Example

is	The condition becomes true if the variables of each side of operator is pointing to the exact same object.	If id(x) and id(y) are equal and x is y, the result is in 1.
is not	The condition become true if the variables of each side of the operator do not point to the same object.	If id(x) and id(y) are not equal and x is not y, the result is not in 1.

Example:

```
#!/usr/bin/example3

x = 10, y = 10

print('x = ', 'x', ':', id(x), 'y = ', 'y', ':', id(y) )

if (x is y)

print(" Both x and y are having same identity ")

else

print(" x and y are not having same identity ")

if( id(x) == id(y) )

print(" Both x and y are having same identity ")

else

print(" x and y are not having same identity ")
```

Output:

x = 10 : 2371593036 y = 10 : 2371593036

Both x and y are having same identity

Both x and y are having same identity

Python Operator Precedence

In the below table, there have all the operators from higher to lower precedence...

Operator	Description
**	Exponentiation(raise to the power)
~ + -	First one is Complement, second is unary plus and last one is unary minus.
/ * % //	Division, multiplication, modulus, floor division
+ -	Addition and subtraction
>> <<	Right bitwise shift and left bitwise shift
&	Bitwise AND
^ |	Bitwise exclusive OR and bitwise regular OR
<= < > >=	Less than equals to, less than, greater than, greater than equals to (comparison operators)

== <> !=	Equality operators
= %= /= //= -= += *= **=	Assignment Operators
is is not	Identity Operators
In not in	Membership Operators
NOT OR AND	Logical Operators

Example:

For example, x = 5 + 14 * 2; in this equation, the value of x is 33, not 38 because the operator * has higher precedence than +. For which it first multiplies 14 * 2 and then add it with 5.

Chapter 3: Basic Variable Types

The variables are used to store data in a programming language. It is possible to store a number or a string in Python as given below:

Example 1.1

Name = "John"

age= 27

weight = 65.4

The = operator is used for assignment of the right value to the variable on the left. Python includes the following basic variable types:

- Numbers
- String
- List
- Tuple
- Dictionary

Example 1.1 has examples for numbers and string, the others will be discussed shortly.

Numbers

Storing a value in a variable is not enough. It is necessary to process the value to have a useful program. The functions or operators in Python are used for this purpose. Basic operators in Python are:

- sum
- difference
- product
- division

It is possible to apply these operators to variables or the numbers directly. The following example shows how to apply the math operations on the numbers directly.

Example 1.2

>>> 2.5 + 3

5.5

>>> 2.5 - 3

-0.5

>>> 2.5 * 3

7.5

>>> 2.5 / 3

0.83

It is also possible to mix a variable and a number:

Example 1.2

>>> x = 2.5

>>> x + 3

5.5

>>> x - 3

-0.5

>>> x * 3

7.5

>>> x / 3

0.83

String

String types are used to store a series of characters as shown in Example 1.1. Note the quotation marks around the characters, which is used to indicate the compiler to interpret this character set as a string. There are operators that works strings. It is possible to use basic math operators on strings as well.

Example 1.3

>>> x = "abc"

>>> x + "d" abcd

>>> x*3

abcabcabc

The + operator is used for concatenation of two strings and the * operator is used for repetition. It is possible to slice the strings:

Example 1.4

>>> name = "John Brown"

>>> name[0]

"John"

>>> name[0 : 4]

"John"

>>> name[5 : 10]

"Brown"

>>> name[5:]

"Brown"

Note that the indexing starts from 0, i.e. the first letter is accessed by x[0] Advanced indexing methods will be discussed in the following Chapters.

Single-Quoted Strings

Let's move on with strings. Try out the following.

>>> "Wild fire is eating away Brazilian Amazon forest."
'Wild fire is eating away Brazilian Amazon forest.'

You might have noticed something odd by now, and that is a change in the quotation marks. The input in the Python shell was in double quotation marks, but the output came in single quotation marks. Let's use single quotation marks this time.

>>> 'Wild fire is eating away Brazilian Amazon forest.'
'Wild fire is eating away Brazilian Amazon forest.'

We have the same result. So, why should we use double quotation marks in the first place? There are some strings that use apostrophes on purpose. So, in order to print those strings in the way we want, we have to use double quotation marks. Let's see how it is done.

>>> 'Wild fire is eating away Brazil's Amazon forest.'
SyntaxError: invalid syntax

Now I will use double quotation marks on the same string.

>>> "Wild fire is eating away Brazil's Amazon forest."
"Wild fire is eating away Brazil's Amazon forest."

You also can use single as well as double quotation marks in the same string.

>>> '"Wild fire is eating away Brazilian Amazon forest." said Brazilian President.'
'"Wild fire is eating away Brazilian Amazon forest." said Brazilian President.'

That's how we can contain a direct sentence to form a string. Though quotation marks can be tricky at times, they turn out to be quite amazing once you understand their use. An interesting thing about strings is their entertainment of escape characters. By using escape characters, you can do away with double quotation marks in a string which contains an apostrophe.

>>> 'Wild fires are eating away Brazil\'s Amazon forests.'
"Wild fires are eating away Brazil's Amazon forests."

In the above example, the escape character is optional while in the next one it is essential, and the syntax will show an error if we omit the escape character.

>>> "'Wild fires are eating away Brazil\'s Amazon forests.'said the Brazilian President."
"'Wild fires are eating away Brazil's Amazon forests.'said the Brazilian President."

In this example, I have enclosed an apostrophe inside the single quotes and full direct speech inside double quotes.

The str and repr in Strings
You might have noticed by now that when we use double quotation marks, they appear in single quotation marks in the result. Let's try it out by using the print command. In python 3 shell, we write the following script.

>>> print ("Wild fires are eating away Brazilian Amazon forests.")
Wild fires are eating away Brazilian Amazon forests.

I'll use a string of integer, a string of a combination of integer and an alphabet with and without the print command. Let's see the result.

>>> 25000

25000

>>> print 25000L

SyntaxError: Missing parentheses in call to 'print'. Did you mean print(25000L)?

>>> print 25000

SyntaxError: Missing parentheses in call to 'print'. Did you mean print(25000)?

>>> print (25000)

25000

Integers don't need the print command to do away with the single quotation marks.

Multiline Strings

You can create a string that may span from three to four or more lines. Let's see how to do it. To successfully do it, I'll assign the value of the string to a variable x.

>>> a = """Brazil's Amazon is burning.

But the government is busy in cornering their political opponents.

Hope the United Nations does something to tackle this crisis."""

>>> print (a)

Brazil's Amazon is burning.

But the government is busy in cornering their political opponents.

Hope the United Nations does something to tackle this crisis.

You also can use single quotation marks to produce the same results. See below.

>>> a = '''Brazil's Amazon is burning.

But the government is busy in cornering their political opponents.

Hope the United Nations does something to tackle this crisis.'''

```
>>> print (a)
```

Brazil's Amazon is burning.

But the government is busy in cornering their political opponents.

Hope the United Nations does something to tackle this crisis.

If you are looking for creating a long string, Python shell allows its construction. For the purpose, you have to use triple quotes. Remember that this is a little bit different from multiline strings. Let's write the code.

```
>>> print '''Amazon is being consumed by fire in Brazil.
```

It keeps going.

It is not to going to be over anytime sooner.

"We are doing our best" said the president of Brazil.

Nature can be scary.'''

Amazon is being consumed by fire in Brazil.

It keeps going.

It is not to going to be over anytime sooner.

"We are doing our best" said the president of Brazil.

Nature can be scary.

The triple quotes can contain almost everything. You can almost add direct speech, apostrophes and lengthy sentences, and can make it as long as you want to.

Let's try out something more interesting.

```
>>> print (a[5])
```

l

```
>>> print (a[0])
```

B

This tells us that Python strings are like arrays of bytes that tend to represent Unicode characters. You can index the string from right to left means from the end toward the start of the string.

>>> a = "Brazil is climatically moderate country."

>>> print (a[-5])

n

You can check the length of your string anytime with the help of the keyword *len*. Let's see how to do that.

>>> print (len(a))

40

String Methods

Python strings offer a variety of built-in methods that you can use for various purposes. For example, if you have left unintentional or intentional whitespaces in the text of your strings, you can remove these whitespaces by a simple method.

>>> a = " Brazil is climatically moderate country. "

>>> print (a)

 Brazil is climatically moderate country.

>>> print(a.strip())#this will remove the whitespaces that I have left at the beginning or the end of the string.

Brazil is climatically moderate country.

If you have written the string in lower case and want it to be displayed to the users in upper case or vice versa, you can do that by a simple method. Please take a look at the following method.

>>> a = " Brazil is climatically moderate country. "

```
>>> print(a.lower())
```

brazil is climatically moderate country.

```
>>> print(a.upper())
```

BRAZIL IS CLIMATICALLY MODERATE COUNTRY.

You also can replace one word or alphabet in a string with another word of alphabet without writing a completely new string.

```
>>> a = " Brazil is climatically moderate country. "
```

```
>>> print(a.replace("B","F"))
```

Frazil is climatically moderate country.

Let's replace one full word with another one. Please try the sample code on your Python shell.

```
>>> a = " Brazil is climatically moderate country. "
```

```
>>> print(a.replace("Brazil","Egypt"))
```

Egypt is climatically moderate country.

You can also split the string into several substrings if you have used separators in the text. There is a dedicated method for the purpose.

```
>>> a = " Brazil, Egypt, America are climatically moderate countries. "
```

```
>>> print(a.split(","))
```

[' Brazil', ' Egypt', ' America are climatically moderate countries. ']

There is a check method for strings to check if a certain word is in the string or not. This can be useful if you are writing a program and want to check the syntax. Instead of reading the entire code, you can check the specific piece of text.

```
>>> txt = " Brazil, Egypt, America are climatically moderate countries. "
```

```
>>> a = "America" in txt
```

>>> print (a)

True

>>> a = "Pakistan" in txt

>>> print (a)

False

You can also check if a certain word doesn't belong to a particular string.

>>> txt = "Brazil and Egypt are climatically moderate country."

>>> a = "Pakistan" not in txt

>>> print(a)

True

>>> txt = "Brazil and Egypt are climatically moderate country."

>>> a = "Brazil" not in txt

>>> print(a)

False

String Format

Python does not allow simple combination of text and numbers that's why you are planning to create a simple program which allows users to see your name and age. You simply cannot do that in an ordinary, but in an extraordinary way, yes, you can! Let's do it in an ordinary way first.

>>> txt = "My father is" + age

Traceback (most recent call last):

  File "<pyshell#10>", line 1, in <module>

    txt = "My father is" + age

TypeError: can only concatenate str (not "int") to str

These strings can be combined with the help of the format() method. It takes the arguments, formats, and fills them in the string.

>>> age = 75

>>> txt = "My father is {}"

>>> print(txt.format(age))

My father is 75

>>> trees = 60000

>>> txt = "Brazil has {} in its Amazon rainforest"

>>> print(txt.format(trees))

Brazil has 60000 in its Amazon rainforest

I have quoted two different examples for your understanding. In the first one I have put the integer at the end of the string, while in the second example I have inserted it in the middle of the string to further explain the method. An amazing thing about the format method is that it has the potential to take an unlimited number of arguments. Let's see how to do that.

>>> quantity = 10

>>> price = 5

>>> myquotation = "I have {} pieces of cotton shirts which I want to for at {} dollars."

>>> print(myquotation.format(quantity,price))

I have 10 pieces of cotton shirts which I want to for at 5 dollars.

I have added two items to the list. Another amazing thing with the format method is that you can shuffle the indices as per your priorities.

>>> quantity = 10

```
>>> price = 5
```

```
>>> myquotation = "My rate is {1} dollars for the {0} pieces of cotton
shirts that I have in my possession."
```

```
>>> print(myquotation.format(quantity,price))
```

My rate is 5 dollars for the 10 pieces of cotton shirts that I have in my possession.

Some additional string methods. If you forgot to capitalize the first letter of the piece of text that you want your users to see, you can edit it by the following string method.

```
txt = "i have 5 pieces of cotton shirts which I want to for at 10 dollars."
```

```
>>> a = txt.capitalize()
```

```
>>> print(a)
```

I have 5 pieces of cotton shirts which i want to for at 10 dollars.

If your string is in uppercase, you can convert it into the lowercase by running a single method in the Python shell.

```
>>> txt = "Brazil and Egypt are climatically moderate country."
```

```
>>> a = txt.casefold()
```

```
>>> print(a)
```

brazil and egypt are climatically moderate country.

Also, you can change the position of the string and bring it in the center of the screen if you want it to be displayed as such to the end user.

Raw Strings, Long Strings & Unicode

Raw strings don't give much consideration to backslashes which otherwise are necessary for inserting elements into a string that would not otherwise have been possible to do. Now we already know that backslashes have a special role in ordinary strings. They enable you to escape things in addition to letting you insert extraordinary elements into the string. But sometimes you just don't this extra service from the Python shell. You are after something else. For example, if you want the string to have a backslash when you are writing path name of a file, you won't want backslash to play its traditional role.

Put it this way. You want to escape the escape characters. So, how do you do it? Let's see.

```
>>> path = 'D:\nowhere'
>>> path
'D:\nowhere'
>>> print path
D:
owhere
>>> print 'D:\\nowhere'
D:\nowhere
```

In the first line, I couldn't escape the escape character. But when I used double backslashes, I am able to escape the escape character itself. There is no new line this time. All went well. This good to write path names, but I have something better. Use the raw string if you want to stop backslash from getting active.

```
>>> print r':\nowhere'
:\nowhere
```

A raw string helps resolve the problems that backslashes keep producing. Let's see the following example.

```
>>> print r'Brazil\'s Amazon has been burning for two months now.'
Brazil\'s Amazon has been burning for two months now.
```

(Hetland, 2008)

Dictionaries in Python

Lists are pretty useful when it comes to fill value in a structure. In Python, you can build a dictionary in which you can store values and can refer to each value by name to present it before the user as per need. You might have been familiar with telephone directory in your home. When you need a number, you directly go to the name of the person and can find his or her phone number. You can also search by his address. Ever wonder how much time you consume on that? How much hassle you have to go through to find a single number? Now move on to the word dictionary. Find the word by searching for the first alphabet. Then slowly turn over the leaves and reach your desired word. This also is not an easy task. Ever consulted a thesaurus? It is the same. You have to track down the word by going through the list of alphabets.

Isn't it a pretty arduous task? We have a better option with Python. You can build a structure that is dubbed a mapping. In simple words, we call it a dictionary. There is hardly a particular order in the dictionary. You can develop your own order as needed. The values in a dictionary can be stored as a number, a tuple or a string. Let's create some real dictionaries.

```
>>> mydict = {

        "car1": "Ferrari",

        "car2": "BMW",

        "car3": "Prius",

        "car4": "Toyota",

        "year": 2008

        }
>>> print(mydict)
```

{'car2': 'BMW', 'car3': 'Prius', 'car1': 'Ferrari', 'car4': 'Toyota', 'year': 2008}

You can access individual items from the dictionary with the help of a simple keyword. Let's roll on.

```
>>> x = mydict["year"]

>>> print(x)

2008

>>> x = mydict["car1"]

>>> print(x)

Ferrari

>>> x = mydict["car4"]

>>> print(x)

Toyota
```

An interesting thing is that you can also do the same job by using a method that is indeed more impressive than a simple keyword.

```
>>> x = mydict.get("year")

>>> print(x)

2008
```

(Python Dictionaries, n.d)

Let's create a little database.

```
>>> carnames = ['BMW', 'Ferrari', 'Toyota', 'Prius']

>>> carnumbers= ['1', '2', '3', '4']

>>> carnumbers[carnames.index('Prius')]

'4'

>>> carnames[carnumbers.index('2')]

'Ferrari'
```

```
>>> carnumbers[carnames.index('Toyota')]
```

'3'

I have created two lists. Then I tried to access the items first by entering names then by numbers. The results are amazing. The dictionary has enabled me to search out items both ways, which is easy and fast. Let's take a look at the basic dictionary operators.

```
>>> mydict = {

        "car1": "Ferrari",

        "car2": "BMW",

        "car3": "Prius",

        "car4": "Toyota",

        "year": 2008

        }
>>> print(len(mydict))
```

5

We can add items on the list with the help of operators.

```
>>> mydict["car5"]= "Lamborghini"
>>> print(mydict)
```

{'car2': 'BMW', 'car3': 'Prius', 'car1': 'Ferrari', 'car4': 'Toyota', 'car5': 'Lamborghini', 'year': 2008}

Yes, you guessed it right. If you can add items, you certainly can remove items from the dictionary.

```
>>> mydict.pop("car4")
```

'Toyota'

```
>>> print(mydict)
```

{'car2': 'BMW', 'car3': 'Prius', 'car1': 'Ferrari', 'car5': 'Lamborghini', 'year': 2008}

The following hollow pop operator will delete a random value from the dictionary. In Python 3, it will delete the last item in your dictionary.

```
>>> mydict.popitem()
```

('car2', 'BMW')

```
>>> print(mydict)
```

{'car3': 'Prius', 'car1': 'Ferrari', 'car5': 'Lamborghini', 'year': 2008}

Now let's delete the dictionary by a single operator.

```
>>> del mydict
```

```
>>> print(mydict)
```


Traceback (most recent call last):

  File "<pyshell#49>", line 1, in <module>

    print(mydict)

NameError: name 'mydict' is not defined

```
>>>
```

You are seeing this error because your dictionary has already been deleted. Now let's rebuild the dictionary and then clear it.

```
>>> mydict = {

        "car1": "Ferrari",

        "car2": "BMW",

        "car3": "Prius",

        "car4": "Toyota",
```

```
    "year": 2008

    }
>>> mydict.clear()

>>> print(mydict)

{}
```

Let's move on to nested dictionaries.

```
>>> mydict = {

    "mycars" : {

    "car1": "Ferrari",

    "car2": "BMW",

    },

    "myusedcars" : {

    "car3": "Prius",

    "car4": "Toyota",

    "year": 2008

    },

    }
>>> print(mydict)
```

{'mycars': {'car2': 'BMW', 'car1': 'Ferrari'}, 'myusedcars': {'car3': 'Prius', 'car4': 'Toyota', 'year': 2008}}
It is important to mention here that key types can be a floating-point, an integer, a string, a number, or a tuple. Also, you can assign any key some value.

(Heland, 2008)

Reading Input and Printing

Python has two important functions for printing the variables and reading them from keyboard, namely *print(), input()* . An example that reads the user's name and prints given below:

Example 2.1

```
name =
input("What is your
name?")

surname =
input("What is your
surname?")

print("Your name is: " + name + surname)
```

The program asks the user for his/her name and surname, then prints the combined name immediately.

The following program is a metric converter from centimeters to inches

Example 2.2

```
cm_inch
= 0.3937

cm =
input("E
nter a
value in
cm.: ")

cm = double(cm)
```

```
inch = cm *
cm_inch

print(f"{cm}
centimeters is
{inch} inches")
```

Chapter 4: Logical Thinking & Data Sets

Most of the programs require a way to decide what to do depending on the different situations. The **if..else** statements are used as decision mechanisms in Python. The following example demonstrates a program that prints an output depending on the value of the variable.

Example 3.1

number =7
if number <5
  print ("Input number is less than 5")
if number >5
  print ("Input number is greater than 5")
if number == 5:
  print("Input number is equal to 5.")

The example will output:

Input number is greater than 5.
Since the number is already set to 7.

Python Data Types

In programming, variables can only store data if you have properly defined the data type. There is more than one type and each type has different functions. You know there are different types of data, like text and numbers. That's why there are different

- If your data is in the form of text, you will use *str* as the keyword so that Python shell may understand what you are trying to enter as information.

- The keyword *dict* is used to enter information in the form of mapping. It is used to store dictionaries. There will be a dedicated section on dictionaries in the upcoming chapters.

- If you have to fill in the code with numbers. You can use *int, complex* and *int* keywords so that Python the information.

- For Boolean type data, use the keyword *bool*.

- For the data that are in the shape of sequence, you can use the following keywords: *range, list* and *tuple*.

- For entering data in the form of sets, you can use *set* and *frozenset*.

- For binary type data, you can use the following keywords: *bytearray, bytes* and *memoryview*.

An interesting thing about Python is that it tells you the data type of any piece of information that you enter in the shell prompt. Let's see how to do it.

>>> x = 5

>>> print(type(x))

<class 'int'>

>>> x = "John"

>>> print(type(x))

<class 'str'>

>>> x = 5.5

>>> print(type(x))

<class 'float'>

>>> x = 1h

SyntaxError: invalid syntax (<pyshell#7>, line 1)

```
>>> x = "1h"
>>> print(type(x))
<class 'str'>
>>> x = False
>>> print(type(x))
<class 'bool'>
>>> x = true
Traceback (most recent call last):
  File "<pyshell#12>", line 1, in <module>
    x = true
NameError: name 'true' is not defined
>>> x = True
>>> print(type(x))
<class 'bool'>
>>> x = a"Hi"
SyntaxError: invalid syntax (<pyshell#15>, line 1)
>>> x = ["BMW", "Ferrari", "Mercedes Benz", "Lamborghini"]
>>> print(type(x))
<class 'list'>
>>> x = ("BMW", "Ferrari", "Mercedes Benz", "Lamborghini")
>>> print(type(x))
<class 'tuple'>
>>> x = {"BMW", "Ferrari", "Mercedes Benz", "Lamborghini"}
>>> print(type(x))
```

```
<class 'set'>
>>> x = {"carname" : "BMW", "carname2" : "Ferrari"}
>>> print(type(x))
<class 'dict'>
>>> x = frozenset({"BMW", "Ferrari", "Mercedes Benz",
"Lamborghini"})
>>> print(type(x))
<class 'frozenset'>
>>>
```

In the above example, I have assigned the variable x different type of values and then I ran the print command to know about the type of each data. At some points, I deliberately entered information in the wrong form so that you may know how to enter information the correct way. For example, you need to put the text inside double quotation marks. Otherwise, it would return the error message. Now, let's see how we can specify a data type in Python shell.

```
>>> x = str("BMW")
>>> print(x)
BMW
>>> x = int(55)
>>> print(x)
55
>>> x = bool(100)
>>> print(x)
True
>>> x = float(55.55)
```

```
>>> print(x)

55.55

>>> x = list(("BMW", "Ferrari", "Mercedes Benz"))

>>> print(x)

['BMW', 'Ferrari', 'Mercedes Benz']

>>> x = tuple(("BMW", "Ferrari", "Mercedes Benz"))

>>> print(x)

('BMW', 'Ferrari', 'Mercedes Benz')

>>> x = set(("BMW", "Ferrari", "Mercedes Benz"))

>>> print(x)

{'Mercedes Benz', 'Ferrari', 'BMW'}

>>> x = dict(carname = "BMW", make = 2005)

>>> print(x)

{'carname': 'BMW', 'make': 2005}

>>>
```

(Python Data Types, n.d)

Python Sets

A set is generally a collection of unordered, as well as unindexed, pieces of data. You have the freedom to write Python sets in curly brackets. Let's navigate through the Python sets to see how they work and help programmers increase their output. We will be creating a simple set as an example.

```
>>> thisset = {"BMW", "Ferrari", "Mercedes Benz", "Toyota", "Lamborghini"}

>>> print(thisset)
```

{'Lamborghini', 'BMW', 'Mercedes Benz', 'Ferrari', 'Toyota'}

>>>

It is important to note that sets are pretty much unordered, that's why you cannot be sure about the order in which they appear. You can see from the above example code that all the car names have changed their position. In fact, the set has pushed the value that was at the end to the forefront of the set. It is a complete upside down of the set. But that's their natural behaviour. Let's move on now to access items from the set. It is something exciting that allows you to ask for certain values from the set.

How to Access Items in a Set

Accessing items from a set is different from accessing an item from a list. We already know that sets don't have any index. They are unordered so you cannot just refer to the index, but you can craft a loop through the entire set. A for loop will run through the depths of the set and come back with the value you needed. In the upcoming code snippet, I'll attempt to create a for loop that will run through the set and print the values that I needed.

```
>>> thisset = {"BMW", "Ferrari", "Mercedes Benz", "Toyota",
"Lamborghini"}

>>> for x in thisset:

        print(x)

Lamborghini

BMW

Mercedes Benz

Ferrari

Toyota

>>>
```

Checking Different Values in a Set

The for loop has displayed individual values from the set. Now I will check the presence of items in the set and see whether they are there or not. The return value is in the form of Booleans, namely True and False. If the value is in the set, you will get the True answer. Otherwise, the answer will be false. One important thing to keep in mind is that if you misspell a value, it will not show syntax error, but will simply return the False option. So, be careful with the spelling or you will misunderstand the response. Ignoring the spelling, you will take it as a real false and decide that the value is not there in the set. Let's see how it works.

>>> myset = {"BMW", "Ferrari", "Mercedes Benz", "Toyota", "Lamborghini", "Rolls Royce", "Baleno", "Prius", "Tesla Land Rover"}

>>> print("Balen" in myset)

False

>>> print("Baleno" in myset)

True

>>> print("BMW" in myset)

True

>>> print("BM" in myset)

False

>>> print("Tesla Land Rover" in myset)

True

>>> print("Jet" in myset)

False

>>> print("Rolls Royce" in myset)

True

```
>>> print("Rolls Royace" in myset)

False

>>> print("Lamborghini" in myset)

True

>>> print("Ferrari" in myset)

True

>>> print("Mercedes Benz" in myset)

True

>>>
```

I have deliberately misspelled some words and used values that in reality don't exist in the set. You can see that I have received the False value in return. Now let's move on to other things. After you have successfully created a set, you don't have the power to change the items the set. Instead, you can add more items to the existing set. There is a specific method for the purpose. In fact, there are two different methods for addition. Their usage depends on the number of items you are about to add.

Adding Single and Multiple Items to Sets

For single items you can make use of the add() method while for the addition of more than one item, you can make use of the update() method. Let's see how to do that.

```
>>> myset = {"BMW", "Ferrari", "Mercedes Benz", "Toyota",
"Lamborghini", "Rolls Royce", "Baleno", "Prius", "Tesla Land Rover"}

>>> myset.add("Foxy")

>>> print(myset)

{'Lamborghini', 'Foxy', 'Prius', 'BMW', 'Mercedes Benz', 'Tesla Land
Rover', 'Rolls Royce', 'Baleno', 'Ferrari', 'Toyota'}
```

>>>

Please don't be surprised to see where your foxy has gone. This is the case with the sets. They don't have any order, remember. Now, I'll try on to add multiple items in the set. Let's see how it is done.

>>> myset = {"BMW", "Ferrari", "Mercedes Benz", "Toyota", "Lamborghini", "Rolls Royce", "Baleno", "Prius", "Tesla Land Rover"}

>>> myset.update(["Hybrid", "IV-Tech", "Sandro", "Suzuki", "Honda", "GM Motors", "Audi"])

>>> print(myset)

{'Lamborghini', 'Sandro', 'GM Motors', 'Prius', 'Audi', 'Hybrid', 'IV-Tech', 'Honda', 'BMW', 'Mercedes Benz', 'Tesla Land Rover', 'Rolls Royce', 'Baleno', 'Ferrari', 'Toyota', 'Suzuki'}

>>>

Finding the Length of Sets

Just as it is with lists, you can get length of the set returned by a simple method. The keyword to achieve this objective is *len*. Let's see how it is done. We already have a fully prepared set. All we need is to get the method ready. Let's see how it is done.

>>> myset = {"BMW", "Ferrari", "Mercedes Benz", "Toyota", "Lamborghini", "Rolls Royce", "Baleno", "Prius", "Tesla Land Rover"}

>>> print(len(myset))

9

>>>

Perhaps you need a set which should be void of Baleno, as you don't need them. Will you prepare an entirely new set? Or will you find a new method to just omit Baleno from the set at the same time saving yourself the hassle of preparing a new set just because you don't need an item anymore. Well, thankfully Python offers us the easier way. We have a method for deleting single items from the set. Do you remember my friend Tibay from the introduction? Tibay is without a doubt a Python ninja by now, but there was a time when see didn't know about this particular method, and whenever she had to remove an item from the set, she would just create a new list. To tell the truth, she was really frustrated at times. However, she learned it the hard way. That's why I want you to learn the easy way. Let's see how to do that.

How to Remove Items from the Sets
There are in general two methods for removing items from the set. One is the remove() method while the other is the discar() method. I'll demonstrate both.

>>> myset = {"BMW", "Ferrari", "Mercedes Benz", "Toyota", "Lamborghini", "Rolls Royce", "Baleno", "Prius", "Tesla Land Rover"}

>>> myset.remove("Baleno")

>>> print(myset)

{'Lamborghini', 'Prius', 'BMW', 'Mercedes Benz', 'Tesla Land Rover', 'Rolls Royce', 'Ferrari', 'Toyota'}

>>>

The output doesn't contain Baleno. Congratulations! You have successfully removed Baleno from the set. An important thing to mention here is that if the item you want to delete is not there in the set, you will receive an error message. See the following example.

>>> myset = {"BMW", "Ferrari", "Mercedes Benz", "Toyota", "Lamborghini", "Rolls Royce", "Prius", "Tesla Land Rover"}

>>> myset.remove("Baleno")

Traceback (most recent call last):

  File "<pyshell#35>", line 1, in <module>

myset.remove("Baleno")

KeyError: 'Baleno'

>>>

This is the error message that will always be displayed in case you try to remove something alien.

The Discard Method

Another method to remove items from a list is the discard method. Let's try it on.

>>> myset = {"BMW", "Ferrari", "Mercedes Benz", "Toyota", "Lamborghini", "Rolls Royce", "Prius", "Tesla Land Rover"}

>>> myset.discard("Prius")

>>> print(myset)

{'Lamborghini', 'BMW', 'Mercedes Benz', 'Tesla Land Rover', 'Rolls Royce', 'Ferrari', 'Toyota'}

>>>

As with the remove method, if you try to delete an item that doesn't exist in the set, you will not see an error message on the screen of the Python shell. Let's see how it is done.

>>> myset = {"BMW", "Ferrari", "Mercedes Benz", "Toyota", "Lamborghini", "Rolls Royce", "Baleno", "Prius", "Tesla Land Rover"}

>>> myset.discard("Foxy")

>>> print(myset)

{'Lamborghini', 'Prius', 'BMW', 'Mercedes Benz', 'Tesla Land Rover', 'Rolls Royce', 'Baleno', 'Ferrari', 'Toyota'}

>>>

The Pop() Method

There is a third method, although an indirect one, to remove an item from the set. It is called the pop() method. The only problem with this method is that it will only remove the last item of the set. Another problem, which is not so serious, is that sets are unordered, you know that, so you can't guess which item will get deleted as you run the method on the Python shell. If you can live with that, you can use this method. There are certain sets in Python that are just meant to be downsized with utter disregard to which item is getting kicked off. The pop() is the best choice in that case. Shall we try it on?

```
>>> myset = {"BMW", "Ferrari", "Mercedes Benz", "Toyota",
"Lamborghini", "Rolls Royce", "Baleno", "Prius", "Tesla Land Rover"}

>>> x = myset.pop()

>>> print(x)

Lamborghini

>>> print(myset)

{'Prius', 'BMW', 'Mercedes Benz', 'Tesla Land Rover', 'Rolls Royce',
'Baleno', 'Ferrari', 'Toyota'}

>>> x = myset.pop()

>>> print(x)

Prius

>>> print(myset)

{'BMW', 'Mercedes Benz', 'Tesla Land Rover', 'Rolls Royce', 'Baleno',
'Ferrari', 'Toyota'}

>>> x = myset.pop()

>>> print(x)

BMW
```

```
>>> print(myset)
```

{'Mercedes Benz', 'Tesla Land Rover', 'Rolls Royce', 'Baleno', 'Ferrari', 'Toyota'}

```
>>> x = myset.pop()
>>> print(x)
```

Mercedes Benz

```
>>> print(myset)
```

{'Tesla Land Rover', 'Rolls Royce', 'Baleno', 'Ferrari', 'Toyota'}

```
>>> x = myset.pop()
>>> print(x)
```

Tesla Land Rover

```
>>> print(myset)
```

{'Rolls Royce', 'Baleno', 'Ferrari', 'Toyota'}

```
>>> x = myset.pop()
>>> print(x)
```

Rolls Royce

```
>>> print(myset)
```

{'Baleno', 'Ferrari', 'Toyota'}

```
>>> x = myset.pop()
>>> print(x)
```

Baleno

```
>>> print(myset)
```

{'Ferrari', 'Toyota'}

```
>>>
```

We have seen that each time I invoked the pop() method, it removed an item irrespective of its place in the set. That's how it works.

How to Clear a Set of Values

If you have a set that has become totally useless, you can empty the set by the clear() method. Let's see how it is done.

```
>>> myset = {"BMW", "Ferrari", "Mercedes Benz", "Toyota",
"Lamborghini", "Rolls Royce", "Baleno", "Prius", "Tesla Land Rover"}

>>> myset.clear()

>>> print(myset)

set()

>>>
```

How to Update a Set with New Values

The set has become empty as the result of the execution of this method. This is your one shot to do away with a useless set. One remarkable thing with the clear method is that it only empties the set, but the set still remains intact. You can update it with other values later on. Let me demonstrate.

```
>>> myset.update(["BMW", "Ferrari", "Mercedes Benz", "Toyota",
"Lamborghini", "Rolls Royce", "Baleno", "Prius", "Tesla Land Rover"])

>>> print(myset)

{'Lamborghini', 'Prius', 'BMW', 'Mercedes Benz', 'Tesla Land Rover',
'Rolls Royce', 'Baleno', 'Ferrari', 'Toyota'}

>>>
```

Deleting a Set

I have successfully updated the set once again. Now let's move on to another method of sets. You can delete the set once and for all by executing a method. This is very fast, as well as dangerous. While you can easily remove loads from the system, you can run the risk of losing some precious data if you don't take immense care. What is immense care means is some checks and confirmations before you run the method. Let's try it on.

```
>>> myset = {"BMW", "Ferrari", "Mercedes Benz", "Toyota",
"Lamborghini", "Rolls Royce", "Baleno", "Prius", "Tesla Land Rover"}
```

```
>>> del myset
```

```
>>> print(myset)
```

Traceback (most recent call last):

  File "<pyshell#72>", line 1, in <module>

    print(myset)

NameError: name 'myset' is not defined

```
>>>
```

You can see that the Python shell has returned an error message: *myset* is not defined. This happens because there is no such method in the Python shell.

Note: It is important that you run this method on a dummy set for testing purposes. Otherwise, you will not be able to retrieve important data.

How to Combine Two Sets

Python sets offer you the flexibility to pair up two sets. To achieve this objective there is actually more than one method. So, let's try them out one by one. On top of the list is the union() method that returns a new set that contains the items from both sets. It perfectly blends the two sets into one another.

```
>>> myset = {"BMW", "Ferrari", "Mercedes Benz", "Toyota",
"Lamborghini", "Rolls Royce", "Baleno", "Prius", "Tesla Land Rover"}
```

```
>>> yourset = {"Harley Davidson", "BMW Motorbike", "Kawasaki",
"Suzuki Heavy Bike"}
```

```
>>> comboset = myset.union(yourset)
```

```
>>> print(comboset)
```

{'Lamborghini', 'Prius', 'BMW Motorbike', 'Suzuki Heavy Bike', 'BMW',
'Mercedes Benz', 'Tesla Land Rover', 'Kawasaki', 'Harley Davidson',
'Rolls Royce', 'Baleno', 'Ferrari', 'Toyota'}

```
>>>
```

It perfectly blended both sets disregarding the order. Now we will
try another method to pair up different sets. Let's see.

```
>>> myset = {"BMW", "Ferrari", "Mercedes Benz", "Toyota",
"Lamborghini", "Rolls Royce", "Baleno", "Prius", "Tesla Land Rover"}
```

```
>>> yourset = {"Harley Davidson", "BMW Motorbike", "Kawasaki",
"Suzuki Heavy Bike"}
```

```
>>> myset.update(yourset)
```

```
>>> print(myset)
```

{'Lamborghini', 'Prius', 'BMW Motorbike', 'Suzuki Heavy Bike', 'BMW',
'Mercedes Benz', 'Tesla Land Rover', 'Kawasaki', 'Harley Davidson',
'Rolls Royce', 'Baleno', 'Ferrari', 'Toyota'}

```
>>>
```

In this case we have updated *myset*. It gained the values of *yourset*.
This doesn't mean the second set loses its value. Let's check the
status of *yourset*.

```
>>> print(yourset)
```

{'Harley Davidson', 'BMW Motorbike', 'Suzuki Heavy Bike', 'Kawasaki'}

```
>>>
```

The following method displays the difference between the two sets. The result of this method will only show the items that are the part of myset and not of yourset. Let's see.

>>> myset = {"BMW", "Ferrari", "Mercedes Benz", "Toyota", "Lamborghini", "Rolls Royce", "Baleno", "Prius", "Tesla Land Rover"}

>>> yourset = {"Harley Davidson", "BMW Motorbike", "Kawasaki", "Suzuki Heavy Bike"}

>>> diffset = myset.difference(yourset)

>>> print(diffset)

{'Lamborghini', 'Ferrari', 'Tesla Land Rover', 'BMW', 'Mercedes Benz', 'Rolls Royce', 'Prius', 'Baleno', 'Toyota'}

>>>

The Intersection of Two Sets

A special method of sets allows you to get an intersection of the two sets. It means the resultes set will contain the items that are parts of both sets. Let's see how it is done.

>>> myset = {"BMW", "Ferrari", "Mercedes Benz", "Toyota", "Lamborghini", "Rolls Royce", "Baleno", "Prius", "Tesla Land Rover"}

>>> yourset = {"Harley Davidson", "BMW Motorbike", "BMW", "Kawasaki", "Suzuki Heavy Bike"}

>>> interset = myset.intersection(yourset)

>>> print(interset)

{'BMW'}

>>>

There can be no intersection at all.

```
>>> myset = {"BMW", "Ferrari", "Mercedes Benz", "Toyota",
"Lamborghini", "Rolls Royce", "Baleno", "Prius", "Tesla Land Rover"}

>>> yourset = {"Harley Davidson", "BMW Motorbike", "Kawasaki",
"Suzuki Heavy Bike"}

>>> interset = myset.intersection(yourset)

>>> print(interset)

set()

>>>
```

The result is an empty set.

Creating a Copy of your Set

You can create a perfect copy of the set by using a simple method. This is helpful because it saves you from the hassle of rewriting entire sets. Instead. it produces perfect copies of them. See how to do that.

```
>>> myset = {"BMW", "Ferrari", "Mercedes Benz", "Toyota",
"Lamborghini", "Rolls Royce", "Baleno", "Prius", "Tesla Land Rover"}

>>> y = myset.copy()

>>> print(y)

{'Lamborghini', 'Prius', 'BMW', 'Mercedes Benz', 'Tesla Land Rover',
'Rolls Royce', 'Baleno', 'Ferrari', 'Toyota'}

>>> print(myset)

{'Lamborghini', 'Prius', 'BMW', 'Mercedes Benz', 'Tesla Land Rover',
'Rolls Royce', 'Baleno', 'Ferrari', 'Toyota'}

>>> print(y)

{'Lamborghini', 'Prius', 'BMW', 'Mercedes Benz', 'Tesla Land Rover',
'Rolls Royce', 'Baleno', 'Ferrari', 'Toyota'}
```

>>>

You can see that now we have two copies of the same set. You can create more. We have another method that returns values in the form of Booleans upon asking if values of one set can be found in the other or not. Let's see how to do that.

>>> myset = {"BMW", "Ferrari", "Mercedes Benz", "Toyota", "Lamborghini", "Rolls Royce", "Baleno", "Prius", "Tesla Land Rover"}

>>> yourset = {"Harley Davidson", "BMW Motorbike", "Kawasaki", "Suzuki Heavy Bike"}

>>> supset = myset.issuperset(yourset)

>>> print(supset)

False

>>>

Now I'll show you if the values of one set are actually found in the other. What happens then?

>>> myset = {"BMW", "Ferrari", "Mercedes Benz", "Toyota", "Lamborghini", "Rolls Royce", "Baleno", "Prius", "Tesla Land Rover", "Harley Davidson", "BMW Motorbike", "Kawasaki", "Suzuki Heavy Bike"}

>>> yourset = {"Harley Davidson", "BMW Motorbike", "Kawasaki", "Suzuki Heavy Bike"}

>>> supset = myset.issuperset(yourset)

>>> print(supset)

True

>>>

The last on the list is the method that helps us transform the values of both sets into perfect symmetry.

```
>>> myset = {"BMW", "Ferrari", "Mercedes Benz", "Toyota",
"Lamborghini", "Rolls Royce", "Baleno", "Prius", "Tesla Land Rover",
"Harley Davidson", "BMW Motorbike", "Kawasaki", "Suzuki Heavy
Bike"}
```

```
>>> yourset = {"Harley Davidson", "BMW Motorbike", "Kawasaki",
"Suzuki Heavy Bike"}
```

```
>>> myset.symmetric_difference_update(yourset)
```

```
>>> print(myset)
```

```
{'Lamborghini', 'Prius', 'BMW', 'Mercedes Benz', 'Tesla Land Rover',
'Rolls Royce', 'Baleno', 'Ferrari', 'Toyota'}
```

```
>>>
```

The method just removed duplication and brought the two sets in
complete symmetry. (Python Sets, n.d)

Chapter 5: Introduction to Loops

Loops are a fundamental concept of programming. The best way to understand loops is to imagine it to be a computer's way of practicing a routine. In any programming language, a Loop allows you to continuously re-iterate a piece of code multiple times without having to write the code every single time.

The general syntax of a loop in Python is as follows.

Syntax

loop condition:

body

Loops are control structures or conditional statements. The conditions structuring a loop tell the computer when the loop needs to be executed and for how long. This condition is what we call the loop condition. The statements or lines of code that you write inside a loop for it to execute is called the loop body. It can be a single statement or a block of code with multiple statements in it.

For example, the phrase "Hello World" can be displayed on a screen 10 times by implementing the print statement each time or by simply using a loop to do the same.

A code bearing the print statement 10 times would look as follows.

```
print ("Hello World")
print ("Hello World")
print ("Hello World")
print ("Hello World")
print ("Hello World")
print ("Hello World")
print ("Hello World")
print ("Hello World")
print ("Hello World")
print ("Hello World")
```

When the above code is executed, the result produced would look like this.

Hello World!
Hello World!
Hello World!
Hello World!
Hello World!
Hello World!
Hello World!
Hello World!
Hello World!
Hello World!

Now, let's try to get the same result using a loop. Re-writing the code to using a loop instead of a writing a print statement each time.

```
count = 0;
while count < 10 :
    print ("Hello World!")
    count += 1
```

The execution of the code above produces the following result.

Hello World!
Hello World!
Hello World!
Hello World!
Hello World!
Hello World!
Hello World!
Hello World!
Hello World!
Hello World!

The same result was obtained with fewer lines of code. We simply wrote a four-line code instead of writing a print statement 10 times. Writing a print statement 10 times may seem simple enough, but imagine when the code gets bigger and more complex. Would you want to write a print statement 100 times if that was the requirement? We could still have the computer print our phrase 100 times with just changing a few numbers on our four-line code. Here's how:

```
count = 0;
while count < 100 :
   print ("Hello World!")
   count += 1
```

Executing the above code would give you a result with the phrase 'Hello World!' printed on your screen 100 times. We obtained the result without writing a print statement 100 times. Loops help the computer run the same code like clockwork based on the conditions we set.

Types of Loops
There are different types of loops in every programming language. Python has two.
1. While loops
2. For loops

In Python, there are many ways that these two loops can be used. For instance, we could use nest loops, loop control statements, use the else, pass, break, and continue statements with loops to name a few.

While Loop: A while loop continues to execute itself if the condition is TRUE and for as long as the condition remains TRUE.
For Loop: A for loop executes itself in a sequential manner. In simpler terms, it iterates over a given sequence of code for the specified number of times.

While Loop

A while loop is a conditional loop. It executes itself if the specified condition is TRUE, and continues to do so for as long as the condition is TRUE.

Syntax

while (loop condition):
> loop body

Indentation is very important in Python, and this is especially true when it comes to loops. The loop body is uniformly indented to the right of the line and holds the loop condition. Remember, Python uses indentation to be able to tell blocks of code apart.

How a While Loop Works

A *while* loop works like the *if*-statement. If the loop condition is TRUE, it executes the loop. Now, it continues to re-iterate the loop until it reaches a point where the condition is FALSE. Python evaluates the loop condition after every single execution. If it finds the condition to be TRUE again, then it re-executes itself. The loop is terminated if the condition is FALSE.

Let us take a look at a few examples of *while* loops.

TASK: *Write a code that prints numbers from 1 through 10 on a new line with and without a loop.*

Printing numbers from 1 through 10 without using a loop would require a *print* statement for each number and our code would look as follows:

#Writing a new print statement for each number on a new line

print ("1")
print ("2")
print ("3")
print ("4")

```
print ("5")
print ("6")
print ("7")
print ("8")
print ("9")
print ("10")
```

This would produce the following result.

```
1
2
3
4
5
6
7
8
9
10
```

Re-writing our code using a *while* loop.

```
#Setting an initial counter

count = 1

#Writing the while condition which iterates the body

#while the counter is less than or equal to 10.

while (count <= 10):
        print (count)
        count +=1
```

On running the above code, the result displayed will be the same as the one with a separate *print* statement on each line. Only this time, we wrote fewer lines of code.

Infinite Loops

Single statement *while* block

A *while* loop that holds only a single line of code in its body.

TASK: Write a code that says 'Hi!' only if the flag is set to 1.

Our loop condition works exactly like an *if* statement.

#Setting an initial variable flag with value 1.
flag = 1
#Writing the loop condition and body which executes the loop
 # for as long as the flag value is found to be 1.
while (flag == 1):
*   print ("Hi!")*

Notice that the loop body holds only a single line of code. Hence it's called a 'single statement *while* block'.

Now try running the above code. What happens?

You're going to see that the computer continuously prints 'Hi!' on a new line and does not stop. Think about why it is behaving in this manner.

Remember, a *while* loop checks for the condition to be true each time it runs through the loop. In the above code, the flag is only set to 1. So when the computer checks the condition after an execution, it always finds the value to be TRUE. Thus, it never knows when to stop. Press *Ctrl + C* to kill an *infinite*-loop.

Python evaluates the condition to be TRUE or FALSE after every iteration of the loop. If a *while*-loop never meets a FALSE state, it results in an **infinite loop.** There may be times in your programming career when infinite loops may be what you need. They are commonly used for programs that are continuously running until they are forced a stop. For example, a web server, or a boomerang video.

For Loops

As stated earlier, a *for* loop executes its body in a sequential manner. A *for* loop is commonly used to traverse through a sequence like a list, an array, or a string.

Syntax

for iterating_var in sequence:
      statement(s)

The *for* loop is especially useful when you want to do something a specific number of times. It is a control structure that terminates itself after it is done iterating over the specified sequence.

Traversing through a String

<u>TASK</u> Write a code that prints every letter of the word 'COMPUTER' using a *for*-loop.

The *for* loop can traverse through any sequence including a list. The task specifically asks to use the *for*-loop.

```
# 'each' is the iterating variable for the string
for each in 'COMPUTER':
        print(each)
```

When the above code is executed, the following result is produced on your screen.

```
C
O
M
P
U
T
E
R
```

For loops can also be used with lists, arrays, or any sequence of the kind. Below is an example of using a *for* loop to traverse through a list.

TASK: Write a code that prints every name in the following list using a *for* loop: Harry, Sam, Mary, John, Jack, Linda, Rachel.

#declaring a list called 'names' that holds all the names.
names = ("Mary", "Sam", "Mary", "John", "Jack", "Linda", "Rachel")
 # 'each' is the iterating variable of the list called names.
for each in names:
        print(each)

On running the above code and the result executed should look as follows.

Mary
Sam
Mary
John
Jack
Linda
Rachel

The Range Function

Python has a built-in function called *range()*. It is ommonly used with *for*-loops. It tells Python to traverse through the specified range in the list. The *range()* function generates a list of integers with the specified range. An important thing to remember is the *range()* function in Python is zero-based like the index, which means that it starts to count from 0.

Python's Range Parameters

Python's *range( )* function can take up to three parameters. Each parameter it takes serves a different purpose. They are generally defined as *stop, start,* or *step*.

Single Parameter

When the function is holding a single parameter, it is holding the *stop* parameter. So with range (stop), stop would be stopping number. Recall that the range function starts from 0, which means it would create an array of whole numbers that start from 0 up to the stopping number but not including the stopping number. So, *range(n)* would generate a list of integers from *0* to *n-1*.

Syntax

range(stop)

Here is an example to help you understand the concept better.

<u>TASK:</u> Print numbers from 0 through 10.

There are multiple ways to obtain the desired result. Let's go over the possible solutions for the above problem from what we have learned so far.

One of the ways to do would be to write out 11 separate print statements. Another way to do so would be to use a counter with a while loop. We could also just use the for loop to print the numbers out or we could use the range( ) function with the for-loop.

Let's first try and write the code using just the for loop without the range( ) function. We would first need to declare a list with all the numbers and then traverse through the list using the loop.

```
#declaring the list.
x = [ 0, 1, 2, 3, 4, 5, 6,7,8,9,10]
for each in x:
        print(each)
```

This would then produce the following result.

0
1
2
3
4
5
6
7
8
9
10

Now, let us try to achieve the same result using the range( ) function. This time we do not need to write the entire list of numbers. We could simply declare a variable for the range function.

i = range(11) #This creates a list 'I' that holds numbers 0 through 10.
for each in i: #We now use the for loop to print each number in the list.
        print(each)

Now try running the above code. It executes the same result as it did before. The range( ) function simplifies a programmer's job.

Note that we use range(11) to print numbers 0 through 10. Remember that range( ) function is zero-based. So, range(11) would print numbers up to 11 but **not** 11.

Double Parameters

What do we do if we wanted to start at 1 instead of 0?

Another method to use the *range( )* function is by passing two parameters to the function. When the function reads only two parameters, it reads them as the *start* and *stop* parameters. The *start* parameter tells the computer where the sequence would **start**, and *stop* tells it where to **end.** Remember, it only goes up to the *stop* parameter, but does **not** include the same.

Syntax

range(start, stop)

TASK: **Print numbers from 1 through 10 using the *range( )* function.**

Our approach would be very similar to the previous one. Only this time, we add a *start* parameter. Let us write the code using this, and see what result we obtain.

#Declaring a variable that will hold the list with the specified range.
x = range (1, 11)# 1 is the starting integer, and 11 would define the stopping point.
#The list will not include 11.
> *for each in x:*
> *print (each)*

When you run the above code, it produces the following result.

1
2
3
4
5
6
7
8
9
10

Notice that it starts to print from 1 up to 10, but does **not** include 11.

Triple Parameters

What if I wanted to print all even numbers between 1 and 10?

Python's *range( )* function can take up to three parameters. When the function has passed three parameters, it reads them as *start, stop*, and *step* in that order. We already learned what the *start* and *stop* parameters do. The *step* parameter is the difference between each number in the sequence.

Syntax

range(start, stop, step)

TASK: Print all even numbers between 1 and 10 using the *range( )* function.

Now, think about the solution for a minute. We need to print only the even numbers. We know that the first even number is 2, and we also know that the difference between two consecutive even numbers is 2.

#Our list would start at 2, and the stopping parameter would be 11.
#The step parameter would be 2.
x = range(2, 11, 2)
#Now writing our for-loop.
for each in x:
        print(each)

Now execute the above code. The result displayed should be as follows.

2
4
6
8
10

Iterating by Sequence Index

Python allows us to use the index of elements to iterate a given sequence. The element's index is used as a counter in loops. Let's take a look at an example.

TASK: In the list provided, print the first five numbers in the given list. Be sure to use a loop and the sequence index to obtain your result. a= [1,2,4,5,7,3,5,7,4].

a [1,2,4,5,7,3,5,7,4]
for index in range (5): #we pass 5 as the parameter because we only need the first five.
        print(a[index])

This should produce the following result.

1

2

4

5

7

Nested Loops

Python allows you to use a loop inside a loop. Such loops are called Nested loops. Any type of loop can be nested under another loop. Meaning, a *for*-loop can be inside a *while*-loop or another *for*-loop. A *while*-loop can be nested under a *for*-loop or another *while*-loop. Be sure that the loops are indented correctly. Indentation is very important in Python. Remember, Python uses indentation to tell blocks of code apart.

Syntax

loop condition:
*   loop condition:*
*   statement(s)*
*   statement(s)*

The computer first reads the outer loop and begins to execute it. When traversing through the outer loop, it reaches the inner loop and completely executes the inner loop before continuing to execute the rest of the body of the outer loop.

TASK: Write a code that multiplies all the numbers in the given list that are between 1 and 9 by 10 and then prints their product. After printing all the products, print the line 'No more numbers that are less than 10.' Write your code using nested loops.

x = [3, 23, 56, 4, 30, 5, 11, 34, 6, 1]

There may be multiple approaches to write the code. Remember that the task requires you to use nested loops. You can nest any type of loop inside another loop, but for the sake of this exercise, let's write a *while* loop inside a *for*-loop.

```
x = [3, 23, 56, 4, 30, 5, 11, 34, 6, 1]
for each in x:
        while each < 10:
                print(each * 10)
                break
print ( 'No more numbers that are less than 10.')
```

When you run this code it should produce the following result.

```
30
40
50
60
10
No more numbers that are less than 10.
```

Break

Recall what we learned about *infinite* loops. What do we do if our code results in an *infinite* loop at a point where we don't need it? A simple solution to that is using a *break* statement. A *break* statement does exactly what the name suggests; it breaks the loop. In other words, when a *break* statement tells the computer to exit out of the loop or terminate its execution.

The general syntax for writing a break statement is as follows.

Syntax

```
loop (condition):
        body
        break
```

Now let's re-write the solution to one of our previous exercises using a break statement this time.

Problem: Write a code that says 'Hi!' only if flag is set to 1.

Our loop statement will check for conditions just like an *if* statement would. But unlike an *if* statement, it is not a one-time execution of its body. It continues to execute the loop every time it finds the loop's condition to be TRUE resulting in an infinite loop.

```
#Setting flag to 1
flag = 1
#Writing the loop which checks for flag to bet to 1 and then prints our statement.
#Adding a break statement at the end of the loop body.
while (count==1):
        print("Hi!")
        break
```

Running the above code will display the following result.

Hi!

The phrase is only printed once because the *break* statement *at* the end of our loop body tells the computer to exit out of the loop instead of falling into an infinite-loop.

An *if* statement can be used inside a loop to set a condition.

A *break* statement can follow an *if* statement inside a loop, which can help set a condition for your program to terminate the loop. You can use an *if* statement in the loop body which can help set a condition to break out of the loop. Let's take a look at an example.

TASK: Print all number from one through nine using a *while* loop. Be sure to use a break statement to exit out of the loop.

num = 1; # setting the initial number to 1.

```
while True: # Initializing the loop.
        print (num);  #printing our number.
        num += 1; #adding 1 to the number we just printed.
        if num == 9: # Setting our condition to break out of
the loop using an if statement.
        break
```

The code above produces the following result.

```
1
2
3
4
5
6
7
8
9
```

Let's analyze the code we wrote.

The task needed us to print numbers one through nine. We set the initial number to one. Notice how we simply used *TRUE* for the loop condition. When we do so, the *while* loop will be executed no matter what. If there's a break that exits the loop after a single execution, then the while loop will be executed at least one time. Towards the end of our loop body, we wrote an *if* statement which defined the condition to break out of the loop.

What would happen if you had the condition set for the number to equal 10 or greater than 9? Try to change your code and take a look at what happens when you do so. What do you see? It printed numbers 1 through 10. Do you know why it did so?

Remember that Python traverses through code in order. We have the *print* statement written first, which is then followed by a statement that increments the number. At the end of all this is when we check for the break condition. If you set the break condition to greater than 9 or equal to 10, then it would already have printed out the number first before reaching the *if* statement that tells the computer to break out of the loop.

Continue Statement

We learned about the *break* statement and how it allows us to exit out of a loop. *Continue* is another conditional statement that can be used with loops. When the program reaches a *continue* statement in a loop, it skips its traversal through the rest of the loop's body and starts its traversal again from the *for* or *while* statement. In other words, it returns to the beginning of the loop and starts to re-execute the loop.

Syntax

loop condition:
         statement(s)
                  continue

The following example should help you understand this better.

TASK: Write a code that adds 1 to only the odd numbers between 1 and 10, and then prints its result. Be sure to use a loop and a *continue* statement to reach your result.

```
x = range(1,11)
for each in x:
        if each % 2 == 0:
                continue
        print (each + 1)
```

The above code should produce the following result.

2

4

6

8

10

Pass Statement

Python allows you to write empty control structures. This is done by using the *pass* statement. It allows you to write empty loops, functions, classes, etc. When a *pass* statement is executed, it returns **null,** meaning it's not going to **do anything**. A good use for *pass* statements is to test codes. You can use it in a place where you plan to write more code later, but need to pass the control structure as TRUE to test what has been written already.

Syntax

loop condition:
>   *statement(s)*
>>   *pass*

Let us take a look at an example to understand this concept better.

TASK: Write a code that only prints odd numbers of the list provided. Be sure to use a *pass* statement with a loop in doing so. x = [2, 3, 4, 97, 23, 1, 0]

x = [2, 3, 4, 97, 23, 1, 0]
for each in x:
>   *if each % 2 == 0:*
>>   *pass # do nothing.*
>   *else:*
>>   *print (each)*

The above code should execute the following result.

3
97
23
1

Using Else Statement with Loops

Python allows us to use *else* statements with loops with either loop.

Using *else* statements with *while*-loops

When an *else* statement is used with a *while* loop, it is executed in a fashion very similar to the *if / else* statements. When the loop condition is found to be FALSE, the *else* statement is executed.

Syntax

> while (loop condition):
> > statement(s)
>
> else:
> > statement(s)

Let's explore of an example of this.

TASK: Using a *while* loop and an *else* statement, print all the items contained in the list provided, and print 'The End!' when you reach the end of the list. L = ["Apple", "Orange", "Mango", "Banana"]

```
l = ["Apple", "Orange", "Mango", "Banana"]
i = 0
while i < len( l ):
        print (l[i])
        i += 1
else:
        print ('The End!')
```

When the above code is executed, the result should look as follows.

> Apple
> Orange
> Mango
> Banana
> The End!

NOTE: If you *break* out of a loop, the *else* statement will not be executed.

Using *else* Statements with *for* loops.

An *else*-statement can be used with a *for* loop in a similar fashion. But here, the *else* statement is executed at the end of the *for* loop or immediately after the *for* loop.

Note that just like in *while* loops, the *else* block will not be executed after a *for* loop if the loop is terminated with a *break* statement.

Syntax

for iterating_var in sequence:
> *statement(s)*
else:
> *statement(s)*

Let's take a look at an example to understand the concept better.

TASK: Write a code that prints only the odd numbers in the given list and prints 'There are no further odd numbers in the list' at the end. A = [2, 4, 7, 12, 35, 90, 101, 50].

a = [2, 4, 7, 12, 35, 90, 101, 50]
for each in a:
> *if each % 2 == 1:*
>> *print (each)*
else:
> *print ('No more odd numbers in the list.')*

When you execute the above code, it should produce the following result.

> *7*
> *35*
> *101*
> *There are no further odd numbers in the list.*

Chapter 6: Python Lists & Tuples

A list is an ordered set in which each of its value is represented by an index. These values are termed as elements. List is like a string, which is an ordered set of characters. In lists, the elements can be of any type. These ordered sets like List or string are called sequences.

Examples

There are various ways to create a list.

([these brackets are used]) ("[ ]")

- [1, 2, 3, 4, 5]   - It's a list of five integers

- ["book", "pen", "eraser", "chalk"] – it's a list of four stationary items.

Nested List:- One list can hold another list i.e Nested List

Example : ["batman", 1, [2, 9], 3.7]

Consecutive Intergers: Lists handles the consecutive integers in an ease in python.

Example: [1, 2, 3, 4, 5] → range(1, 5)

This range function consistes of two arguments and delivers a list hoding integers from first argument to second argument.

Note: First argument is encluded in the list whereas second argument is excluded.

Others types of Range Function. Range has two other forms as well.

Three Arguments Range: The third parameter gives the gap between two successive values (also called Step Size)

Let's understand by an example: range(2, 12, 2)

This gives us the list as : [2, 4, 6, 8, 10]

- Single Argument : It creates a list that starts from 0.

Example: [0, 1, 2, 3, 4]

Empty List: It does not contain any value. It is represented by [].

So now we have created our list and we will pass them as an argument to the functions.

Let's understand it by few examples:

room = ["fan", "sofa", "bed"]

Sum = [13, 14]

Print Sum, room

How to Access the Elements

The syntax is same as the syntax for accessing the characters of a string using the bracket operator ([]). Index is represented inside the brackets.

Note: Indices begin from 0.

Example: print sum[2]

        add[1] = 4

The bracket operator can be used anywhere in the expression.

We use loops to access the index

room = ["sofa", "bed", "pillow", "canvas"]

i = 0   // It will iterate for 4 times i.e. 0, 1, 2 and 3 and then it fails

while i < 4:

print room[i]

i = i + 1

Operations in List
The + operator: It concatenates the list.

x = [2,4,6]

y = [1,3,5]

z = x + y

print z => [2, 4, 6, 1, 3, 5]

* operator: It gives the number of time the value needs to be repeated.

Example:

[1] * 4 → [1, 1, 1, 1]

[2, 4, 6] * 2 → [2, 4, 6, 2, 4, 6]

List Slices
It works well with lists. Let us understand by an example.

num = ['1', '2', '3', '4', '5', '6']

→ list[1 : 4]

['2', '3', '4', '5']

→ list[:4]

['0', '1', '2', '3']

→ list[3:]

['4', '5', '6']

→ list[:]

['1', '2', '3', '4', '5', '6']

Mutable Lists

Lists are mutable in nature, which means that we can change their elements.

country = ["India", "France", "Italy"]

>>> country[0] = "USA"

>>> country[1] = "Sudan"

>>> print county → ['USA', 'France', 'Sudan']

We can update several elements at a time.

Example:

list = ['1', '2', '3', '4', '5', '6']

list[1 : 3] = ['a', 'b']

print list

['1', 'a', 'b', '4', '5', '6']

We can likewise expel components from a list by allotting the vacant list to them.

For example:

list = ['1', '2', '3', '4', '5', '6']

list[1 : 3] = []

print list

['1', '4', '5', '6']

List Deletion

It is alternative to slice which can be error-prone. del function removes an element from a list.

For example:

a = ['a', 'b', 'c']

del a[1]

print a

→['a', 'c']

del can handles negative indices_and may lead to runtime error if the index is out of range.

Tuples Introduction

As you all familiar with the list in any other programming language, similarly we have one more data set, which is a tuple. The tuple is similar to a list where we can store multiple types of values either string, integer, float or any other. So if we have a list then why we use a tuple.

Firstly, the value of tuple cannot change. If we defined the value of tuple, then we can modify its value neither in real-time nor on static time. Tuple is used for non-changeable value. For example, suppose you want to make some entries mandatory in your program so none can change its value then defined it in a tuple.

Secondly, item in the list is defined in square brackets [] but in tuple item is defined in parentheses () and separated by commas. For example:

tup = (10, 20, 30, 40, 50)

Empty, Similar, Mixed Tuple:

Here are some examples of the different items that can be held in the tuple. Tup1 has no value its empty tuple; tup2 is the collection of integer items; tup3 has mixed values like integer, string, and float.

Empty Tuple initialize with tup1

tup1 = ()

print(tup1)

Output will be ()

tup2 has integer items

tup2 = (21, 1995, 3)

print(tup2)

Output will be (21, 1995, 03)

tup3 has mixed values

tup3 = (1, "Python", 1.56)

print(tup3)

Output will be (1, "Python", 1.56)

Tuple Packing
Tuple can also be defined without parenthesis it is called tuple packing.

tuple packing

```python
tup = 10, 30, "Packing"

print(tup)

# Output : 10, 30, "Packing"
```

Creating a tuple with one value may give you a different output. For example, creating a tuple with one item and using type method (In Python type is a built-in method, which comes when figuring out the type of the variable used in the runtime) then it gives different types of output. In first without a comma, it gives the item type. With coma and without parenthesis it gives the same output given the type of item that's a tuple.

```python
# Creating a tuple T having one element

T = ("Hi")

print(type(T))

# Output <class 'str'>
```

```python
# With comma

T = ("Hi",)

print(type(T))

# Output <class 'tuple'>
```

```python
# Without parentheses gave the same result which get with comma

T = "Hi",

print(type(T))

# Output <class 'tuple'>
```

Nested Tuple

A tuple can also be a collection of tuples, lists, and string.

For example:

Nested tuple

n_tup = ("Packing", "Making", (1, 2, 3, 4), [10, 20, 30, 40])

print(type (n_tup))

print(n_tup)

Output : <class 'tuple'>

Output : ("Packing", "Making", (1, 2, 3, 4), [10, 20, 30, 40])

Access Values in Tuple

Accessing values in tuple there are different ways to access elements in a tuple:

1.   By Index

Indexing in the tuple is similar than the list we use index operator [] for accessing any item in tuple. The index starts at 0.

If you have tup = (10, 20, 30, 40,) then indexing is:

tup[0] = 10, tup[1] = 20, tup[2] = 30, tup[3] = 40.

If you use tup[4] = 40, then python will give you IndexError: tuple index out of range.

Indices must be in integer not in a string or in a float.

If you use tup[3.1] then it will give you TypeError: tuple indices must be integers, not float.

Similarly, for accessing values in nested tuple tup[0][3], we have to use to indices first for the desired item in nested tuple, second indices for access the value from the desired item. Please have a look at an example to understand more clearly.

```python
# Indices of tuple
tup1 = ('p', 'a', 'c', 'k', 'k', 'k', 'i', 'n', 'g')

print(tup1[0])
# Output: p
print(tup1[4])
# Output: k


print (tup1[10]) # IndexError: tuple index out of range


# Nested tuple
n_tup = ("python", [ 1, 2, 3, 4 ], ( 5, 6, 7,8 ) )
print (n_tup[0][3])
# Output: h
print (n_tup[2][3])
# Output: 8
```

2. By Negative Indices:

In Python we can also access the values by negative indexing. The last value referred to -1, then second last -2 and so on. Below is the example of using indices for both −ve and +ve.

-6 -5 -4 -3   -2 -1

P Y   T   H   O   N

0   1   2   3   4   5

Negative Indices of tuple

```
tup1 = ('p', 'a', 'c', 'k', 'k', 'k', 'i', 'n', 'g')
```

```
print(tup1[-1])
```

Output: g

```
print(tup1[-4])
```

Output: k

3. Slicing:

We can access the range of the elements within the tuple. The operator ":" colon used for slicing the range of elements in the tuple.

Slicing of tuple

```
tup1 = ('p', 'a', 'c', 'k', 'k', 'k', 'i', 'n', 'g')
```

accessing element from 2nd to 5th

```
print(tup1[1:4])
```

Output: ('a', 'c', 'k')

accessing form the beginning to 6th

```
print(tup1[:-4])
```

Output: ('p', 'a', 'c', 'k', 'k')

accessing from 4th to end

```
print(tup1[4:])
```

Output: ('k', 'k', 'i', 'n', 'g')

accessing from beginning to end

print(tup1[:]) #Output: ('p', 'a', 'c', 'k', 'k', 'k', 'i', 'n', 'g')

#print (tup1[10]) #IndexError: tuple index out of range

Updating a Tuple

As we discussed before, the tuple cannot change once it got assigned. But, a nested tuple can change its value if and only if it contains changeable items like a list. For example, whenever we change the value of my_tup it throws an error TypeError: 'tuple' object does not support item assignment. But if we change any value of list defined in nested tuple then it gets changed.

Updating items in tuple

my_tup = (1, 2, 3, 4, 5, 6, [7, 8, 9])

Replacing an item from tuple

my_tup[1]= 10 #TypeError: 'tuple' object does not support item assignment

#However the my_tuple contains list. So we can change an item from list

my_tup[6][0] = 0

print(my_tup)

#Output: (1, 2, 3, 4, 5, 6, [0, 8, 9])

Deleting Tuple

As in the previous topic, we concluded that tuple values cannot be changed. So we cannot delete the items of tuple too. But we can delete a tuple completely.

del keyword is used for deleting the tuple.

Deleting items in tuple

my_tup = (1, 2, 3, 4, 5, 6, [7, 8, 9])

Deleting an item from tuple

del my_tup[1] #TypeError: 'tuple' object doesn't support item deletion

#However we can delete a whole tuple

del my_tup

print(my_tup) #NameError: name 'my_tup' is not defined

#Because the my_tup doesn't exist after deletion.

Type of Operator

'+' - is a concatenate operator. Used to combine the two tuples.

'*' - is a repeat operator. Used to repeat a specific value a specific number of times.

 # Concatenate

tup1 = (1, 2, 3, 4, 5,)

tup2 = 6, 7, 8, 9, 10

tup3 = tup1 + tup2

print (tup3)

Output : (1, 2, 3, 4, 5, 6, 7, 8, 9, 10)

#Repeat

```
print (tup1 * 3)
# Output : (1, 2, 3, 4, 5, 1, 2, 3, 4, 5, 1, 2, 3, 4, 5)
```

Types of Methods

Tuple doesn't support the addition and deletion of items. So we have only two methods.

Methods	Description
count(x)	It gives the number of x items present in tuple
index(x)	It gives the index of first x item present in tuple
len(tuple)	It gives the length of a tuple

```
my_tup = ('p', 'a', 'c', 'k', 'k', 'k', 'i', 'n', 'g')


#Using count method to find out number of k

print(my_tup.count('k'))

# Output: 3


#Using index method to find out index of first a

print(my_tup.index('a'))

# Output: 1


#Using len method to find out length of tuple

print(len(tup))
```

Output: 9

Types of Operation

To find out whether the item exists in a tuple or not, then use keywords either in or not in. The result always comes in true or false.

my_tup = ('p', 'a', 'c', 'k', 'k', 'k', 'i', 'n', 'g')

Using in operator

print('a' in my_tup)

Output: True

print('s' in my_tup)

Output: False

Using not in operator

print('c'in my_tup)

Output: True

To iterate through each item in a tuple, use a for loop:

Mytup= ("packing", "unboxing", "cherry")

for x in Mytup:

print x

#Output

packing

unboxing

cherry

Advantages of Tuple

1. Tuple contains all the mixed values as we studied in our whole article, but the list cannot hold the different data type.

2. Tuple values are non-changeable. Iteration through tuple is fast and boost performance in spite of the list. The values of the tuple are fixed so it can be used as a key for a variable.

3. The data in the tuple is protected due to its unchangeable property.

Chapter 7: Python Exception Handling

Exception Handling is a very important module for any programing language as it helps to manage the runtime and respond to runtime exceptions if any unexpected event happens during the normal flow of the code. It makes sure that the system doesn't crash or becomes unresponsive if an error has come in your program.

Python handles it via 2 methods: Exception Handling and Assertions.

Let us see Assertions first.

Assertions in Python

It helps in the basic check of the program. It works like raise-if and raise if-not statement. The program is tested, and Boolean value is recorded. False statements raise the exception. Let us understand it by a situation. Let say the code is not executing. So, we place print statements before every new function so that we come to know the line up to which the code is running. Now I guess you can relate it easily to assertion.

Syntax:

    assert expression [, argument]

It is good to know that assertion exceptions can be handled by try-catch statements.

What is an Exception?

An exception can be related to an unexpected or unwanted event, which is obtained at the time of execution of program. In other words, it disturbs the normal flow of execution of the program at the run time. Exception to a non-programmer can be related as an instance that does not follow a general rule. It is an object that points towards an error that occurs when the code cannot handle it.

After the exception is generated, it should be handled by our code else it terminates the execution of the program.

For Example:

1)

>>> print 44/0

ZeroDivisionError: integer division or modulo

2)

>>> x = []

>>> print x[4]

IndexError: list index out of range

In the above two examples we are obtaining the error messages with the reason of error. The error message has two parts. Before the colon is the type of error, and after the colon is the detail of the error.

Handling an Exception

If exception is raised there should be a way to handle it. Also, sometimes we wish to execute our code which can cause an exception, but we don't want the execution to terminate. The risk of exception can be handled by using the try and except statements. The **try block** holds the code which fosters the risk of an exception whereas the handling code is posted in the **except block**. The try block executes in the first block and ignores the except block if no exception occurs.

Syntax of try and except:

try:

what needs to be executed

except   Expression1

        if this exception, then execute.

except   Expression2

        if this exception, then execute.

else

        Execute if no exception

But in the above syntax, if we have so many except statements in this fashion then though all the exceptions get generated, it would difficult to understand the root cause of the exception.

Exception Clause with No Exception

When the exception clause is executed and there is no exception, the else part gets executed.

Syntax :

```
try:

        what needs to be executed

except:

        if this exception, then execute.

else:

        execute if no exception
```


Exception Clause with Multiple Exception

We can have multiple except statements for one try statement.

```
try:
```

what needs to be executed

except: (Exception 1 [, Exception2 [, ...Exception x]]]):

if any exception from the above, then execute.

In the given except statement we have many exceptions. The desired one gets executed.

>>> We can use a generic except clause which takes care of all the exception.

>>> The else part executes if no exception is generated by try block.

The Try-Finally Clause
The code in the finally block gets executed irrespective of whether try block generates an exception or not.

try:

what needs to be executed

finally:

will always be executed

Now let's consider an example to sum up all.

>>> Let's try to write in a file to which you only have read permission.


```
try:
 f = open( "python.txt" )   # We have opened the file here
```

```
  f.write( "welcome" )      # We are trying to write in the file here
except:
  print( "Request Denied- You don't have any access" )
finally:
  f.close()            # This line will execute irrespective of try block
```

Arguments in Exception

Whenever an exception is generated, it can have values associated with it. This is called the argument of the exception. Its type depends on the type of exception.

Syntax :

try:

      what has to be executed

except ExceptionType as Argument:

      argument can be printed here

Raising an Exception

It helps the coder to raise the desired exception. The raise statement has two arguments which includes the type of exception and detailed

information about the error. Few examples of type of errors are TypeError, ValueError, KeyError, NotImplementedError, etc.

Example:

```
>>>    def number() :

            x = input ( ' Please enter a number:' )

            if x == 3:

                raise ValueError, '3 is an unlucky number'
```

```
        return x
```

User-Defined Exception

We can create our own exceptions in python. We derive classes from the default built-in exceptions directly or indirectly. These exception classes can function the same as other classes do, but are usually limited to information about error for exception handling.

Let's take an example to understand the concept:

Let the case is about *ValueError*. Hence, we'll create a subclass of it. It helps to portray the desired information when exception is caught.

Let us define a class →

```
        Class Nameerror( ValueError ):

            def_init_( self, arg ):

                self.args = arg
```

Here Nameerror is the new class. Now we'll raise the exception →

```
        try:

            raise Nameerror( 'Poor name' )

        except:

            print e.args
```

Here 'e' creates the instance of the subclass Nameerror.

Chapter 8: The If Statements

It is the basis of programming that involves examination certain conditions and making a decision accordingly. An If statement in Python examines a program and responds accordingly and appropriately. I'll explain in this section how to write If statements and from there I'll go on to write more complex If statements, and see what they can do while you are all set to program. Python supports the following logical conditions.

- a>=b shows greater than or equal to.

- a == b is the sign of equality in Python.

- a<b is the sign of less than.

- a != b is used for showing inequality.

- a <= b shows less than or equal to.

Let's write an If statement.

>>> a = 45

>>> b = 456

>>> if b > a:

    print("b has a greater value than that of a")

b has a greater value than that of a

You can clearly see that there are two variables used in the code. I assigned them two different values that are certainly not equal. Then I tested the inequality through the If statement. When I ran the code in the Python shell, it returned the answer after testing the condition. Python is sensitive to indentation so if you try to slice off indentation, you will get an error. Let's see how it works.

>>> a = 45

```
>>> b = 456

>>> if b > a:

print("b has a greater value than that of a")

  File "<pyshell#8>", line 2

    print("b has a greater value than that of a")

      ^

IndentationError: expected an indented block
```

Now I'll move on to the *elif* keyword. This keyword allows us a greater freedom of choice. If one statement turns out to be false, the second one runs and gives us the result. Let's see how it works.

```
>>> a = 300

>>> b = 40

>>> a = 40

>>> b = 40

>>> if b > a:

        print("b is greater than that of a")

elif a == b:

        print("a has equal value as b")

a has equal value as b
```

Now, we'll move on to the elif-else statement, which gives more freedom of decision-making to your computer. You can add more conditions to expand the logical ability of your machine. Let's see how to write them and execute them accordingly.

```
>>> a = 300

>>> b = 40
```

```
>>> if b > a:

    print("b is greater than that of a")

elif a == b:

    print("a and b are equal")

else:

    print("a has greater value than that of b")

a has greater value than that of b
```

Now let's see if you miss indentation in this code, what happens in the shell.

```
>>> a = 300

>>> b = 40

>>> if b > a:

    print("b is greater than that of a")

elif a == b:

    print("a and b are equal")

    else:


SyntaxError: invalid syntax
```

Indentation can really ruin your code. Whenever you feel that you have written the right code but is still fails to execute, check for the indentation. You will know why are you having problem in running the code.

In the above example, we used elif and else together. You can use else statement separately.

```
>>> a = 300
```

```
>>> b = 40
>>> if b > a:
        print("b is greater than that of a")
else:
        print("a and b are equal")
```

a and b are equal

I have randomly written this statement in the shell. You can change what you want to see in the output.

```
>>> a = 300
>>> b = 40
>>> if b > a:
        print("b is greater than that of a")
else:
        print("a is greater than b")
```

a is greater than b

For those who are using Python 2, you may have to enter twice after the file print option in order to see the result. Python shell takes the first enter as a continuance of the code. It means it understands it as if you want to add more to the if statement. So, just press the *enter* button twice to see the result of your statement.

Another interesting thing about the If statements is that you can write in on one line if you have to write a simple one. Let's see.

```
a = 400
b = 40
if a > b: print("a has greater value than that of b")
```

a has greater value than that of b

We call it the shorthand If statement. Let's move on to the And statement, which offers more flexibility. You can pair up a couple of conditions together to test them simultaneously.

a = 300

b = 43

c = 700

if a > b and c > a:

  print("The two conditions are true.")

The two conditions are true.

We can see that both conditions are true. We have the same printed out on the screen.

a = 300

b = 55

c = 600

if a > b or a > c:

  print("One of the given conditions is definitely True.")

One of the given conditions is definitely True.

An amazing thing with the if statement is that you can nest one inside the other for more complex programming. It is easier to do if you know the right format. Let's do that.

x = 55

if x > 20:

  print("The value is above twenty.")

  if x > 30:

```
   print("The value is also above 30!")

 else:

   print("The value is below 30.")
```

The value is above twenty.

The value is below 30.

(Python if...else, n.d)

Now, I'll move on to discuss functions in Python and their uses. We'll be doing some practical coding along with solutions so that you can learn it by heart. Functions are special items in Python. They save you from writing the same code again and again to building a specific program. Programmers have to perform a certain task again and again while they are building a program. Instead of typing it fresh, you can store the entire code in a function and use it as needed. Using the code that is stored inside a function is called calling a function. Your specific call will tell Python shell to run the same code. In this way, functions offer us speed, ease of use, and an error-free environment.

Each time we write a new code, there is a greater chance of error. All this results in a waste of your precious time. A specific function can only do a special task that you have assigned it. You can write more than one functions. First of all, you have to pass the information to a function then you can store them in separate files dubbed as modules in order to organize the program files. The data that is passed to a function is called parameters. These parameters are returned as a result.

How to Define a Function

Let's create a simple function first to give you the knowledge on how to do that. First of all, the syntax is as under:

```
>>> def azure_sky():

      """Discuss the color of the sky."""
```

```
        print("The sky is turning into azure day by day")
```

>>> azure_sky()

The sky is turning into azure day by day

So, what has happened? I created a function with the help of the keyword 'def' and then I entered its value. The function stored the value and printed it out when I called the function in the second last line. That's how it works always. Python recognizes the function by the keyword *def*. For a simple function like the above one, the parenthesis remains empty. For more complex functions, you need to fill in the parenthesis different values. The definition ends in a colon.

There will be some indented lines after you have defined the function. In one of these lines, you will have to enter a piece of text, which is dubbed as a docstring. This usually describes what a function does. As I have done, you will have to put docstrings inside triple quotes. You miss the quote and it will return error. Python recognizes a docstring by the triple quotes. I wrote the code in the line that started with print. After you have written the code, the time is ripe to call it. So, in the last line I have called the function by just writing the name of the function and putting parenthesis in the end. The parenthesis can be filled with different values to achieve certain programming objectives. A function call can be given any time at any point of a program.

How to Pass Information to a Function

Python functions are amazing in a way that you can pass information to the function. You can modify it anytime by adding words, phrases and even sentences. I have created a function titled as azure_sky(). It has a certain value about the color of the sky. We can add to this information by a simple code. Let's do that.

>>> def azure_sky(info):

```
"""Discuss the color of the sky."""

    print("The sky is turning into azure day by day," + info.title() +
"!")
```

```
>>> azure_sky('But humidity takes its toll on the azure color.')
```

The sky is turning into azure day by day,But Humidity Takes Its Toll
On The Azure Color.!

You can manipulate the information you are passing to the function
with the help of simple commands. For example, you can choose
whether to display the result in the upper case or not. See the
following snippet.

```
>>> def azure_sky(info):

    """Discuss the color of the sky."""

    print("The sky is turning into azure day by day," + info.upper()
+ "!")
```

```
>>> azure_sky('But humidity takes its toll on the azure color.')
```

The sky is turning into azure day by day,BUT HUMIDITY TAKES ITS
TOLL ON THE AZURE COLOR.!

Now I will convert the snippet into lower case. Let's see how to do
that.

```
>>> def azure_sky(info):

    """Discuss the color of the sky."""

    print("The sky is turning into azure day by day," + info.lower()
+ "!")
```

>>> azure_sky('But humidity takes its toll on the azure color.')

The sky is turning into azure day by day,but humidity takes its toll on the azure color.!

So, the Python function smoothly passes the information to the function and also allows programmers the freedom to style the display of the information at will, as we have seen in the code snippets that I have written.

Note: You can use the code snippets that I have given in this book for practice purposes. I have used Python 2 shell to compose these codes. You can also download Python 3 shell, but it has some new features, so some of the codes may not work in it or may display the information that you didn't ask for.

A Look at Function Arguments and Parameters

We have now learned how to write a function program and how to pass additional information to the same. Everything is simple to learn. All it takes is exhaustive practice. I have used *info* as a variable to fill in and pass on the information to the function. This variable is named as *parameter*. When we make a call to the function, we have the additional piece of information displayed as a result. As the variable *info* is called parameter, the value that we place in it is called an argument. In this case, the argument is '*But humidity takes its toll on the azure color.*' Don't make the mistake of blending the two terms together. Parameters and arguments are two different things.

A single function can contain more than one parameters and arguments. Let's try something interesting. I am going to use different arguments for the passing information to the function to have different results.

>>> def azure_sky(carname):

        print(carname + "is one of the super speedy cars in the world")

>>> azure_sky("BMW")

BMWis one of the super speedy cars in the world

```
>>> azure_sky("Ferrari")
```

Ferrariis one of the super speedy cars in the world

```
>>> azure_sky("Lamborghini")
```

Lamborghiniis one of the super speedy cars in the world

All went well. I have successfully passed multiple arguments to the function. But, if you have noticed, I failed to display the information correctly. The helping verb 'is' appears to be combined with the car name in each result. Any clues why this happened? Earlier I told you that Python is highly sensitive about indentation. The same applies here. I failed to take care of proper indentation in this code snippet. Let's do it the right way.

```
>>> def azure_sky(carname):
        print(carname + " is one of the super speedy cars in the world")
```

```
>>> azure_sky("BMW")
```

BMW is one of the super speedy cars in the world

```
>>> azure_sky("Ferrari")
```

Ferrari is one of the super speedy cars in the world

```
>>> azure_sky("Lamborghini")
```

Lamborghini is one of the super speedy cars in the world

You also have the choice of setting a default value for the function. This can be helpful where you have some code that you need to repeat multiple times. So, instead of writing it again and again, you can just invoke the default argument. See the code snippet.

```
>>> def azure_sky(carname = "Mercedes Benz"):
        print(carname + " is one of the super speedy cars in the world")
```

>>> azure_sky("BMW")

BMW is one of the super speedy cars in the world

>>> azure_sky()

Mercedes Benz is one of the super speedy cars in the world

>>> azure_sky("Ferrari")

Ferrari is one of the super speedy cars in the world

>>> azure_sky("Lamborghini")

Lamborghini is one of the super speedy cars in the world

I have invoked the default argument in the middle of the program, and it displayed the value I have put in it. You can call it as many times as you want to. See the following example.

```
>>> def azure_sky(carname = "Mercedes Benz"):
        print(carname + " is one of the super speedy cars in the world")
```

>>> azure_sky()

Mercedes Benz is one of the super speedy cars in the world

>>> azure_sky()

Mercedes Benz is one of the super speedy cars in the world

>>> azure_sky()

Mercedes Benz is one of the super speedy cars in the world

How to Pass a List to the Function as a Parameter

You can prepare a list that you can pass as a parameter to the function. In fact, apart from the list, you can pass on a string, a dictionary, and numbers, etc. to the function. Let's pass on a list to the function.

```
>>> def azure_sky(carname):
        for a in carname:
            print(a)


>>> supercars = ["BMW", "Ferrari", "Mercedes Benz", "Lamborghini"]
>>> azure_sky(supercars)
BMW
Ferrari
Mercedes Benz
Lamborghini
```

You can also use a function to return a value to the Python shell. Let's see how to do that.

```
>>> def azure_sky(x):
        return 25 + x


>>> print(azure_sky(50))
75
>>> print(azure_sky(100))
125
>>> print(azure_sky(125))
150
```

I have used arithmetic addition for returning the value. Each number that I put in the parenthesis is returned after being added into 25. Now, instead of addition, I'll use multiplication and see the results.

```
>>> def azure_sky(x):

        return 35 * x


>>> print(azure_sky(125))

4375

>>> print(azure_sky(5))

175

>>> print(azure_sky(45))

1575
```

You can also send arguments in the following way. Let's see how it is done.

```
>>> def azure_sky(car1, car2, car3, car4):

        print("The super fast car in the world is " + car3)


>>> azure_sky(car1 = "BMW", car2 = "Ferrari", car3 = "Lamborghini",
car4 = "Mercedes Benz")
```

The super fast car in the world is Lamborghini

Let's try another argument.

```
>>> def azure_sky(car1, car2, car3, car4):

        print("The super fast car in the world is " + car1)


>>> azure_sky(car1 = "BMW", car2 = "Ferrari", car3 = "Lamborghini",
car4 = "Mercedes Benz")
```

The superfast car in the world is BMW

In the above, I have defined each argument in the function. There is another way to pass multiple arguments in the function without even defining them. They are dubbed as arbitrary arguments.

```
>>> def azure_sky(*cars):
        print("The super fast car in the world is " + cars[2])
```

```
>>> azure_sky("BMW", "Ferrari", "Lamborghini", "Mercedes Benz")
```

The super fast car in the world is Lamborghini

```
>>> def azure_sky(*cars):
        print("The super fast car in the world is " + cars[3])
```

```
>>> azure_sky("BMW", "Ferrari", "Lamborghini", "Mercedes Benz")
```

The super fast car in the world is Mercedes Benz

You can invoke the other two values by filling in the index number into the square brackets. Remember that the index starts at zero. Allow me to show you.

```
>>> def azure_sky(*cars):
        print("The super fast car in the world is " + cars[0])
```

```
>>> azure_sky("BMW", "Ferrari", "Lamborghini", "Mercedes Benz")
```

The super fast car in the world is BMW

That's how index works. Just start it from zero and so on. (Python Functions, n.d)

Positional Arguments

Moving on with the functions, I'll discuss positional arguments. Upon calling a function, Python needs to match one argument in your function with the parameter that you have defined in the function. It does that on the basis of the order of the arguments. You change the order and the displayed values will be changed. The values that the function matches for you are called positional arguments. They are named as such because they heavily rely on the position of the values you enter in the function. Let's create a function that displays the names of cars and their types.

>>> def azure_sky(car_name, car_type):

    """Display information about supercars and average cars."""

    print("\nI possess a " + car_name.title() + ".")

    print("It is a " + car_type + ".")

It is a fast.

>>> azure_sky('BMW', 'fast car')

I possess a Bmw.

It is a fast car.

>>>

>>> azure_sky('Ferrari', 'supercar')

I possess a Ferrari.

It is a supercar.

>>> azure_sky('Mercedes Benz', 'fast car')

I possess a Mercedes Benz.

It is a fast car.

Python shell displayed the values as I had ordered them in the function. It read the position of the values and displayed them accordingly. I have deliberately used an odd name for the function to show that you can choose any name to define a function. If you want to, you can change the name to describe_cars for an easier understanding. The argument, BMW gets stored in the parameter car_name and the argument fast car is stored in the parameter car_type. In this way you can add more arguments. I'll be defining a function that will have four parameters. But first, I'll show you what happens when you change the order number in the arguments section.

```
>>> def azure_sky(car_name, car_type):

        """Display information about supercars and average cars."""

        print("\nI possess a " + car_name.title() + ".")

        print("It is a " + car_type + ".")

>>> azure_sky('fast car', 'BMW')
```

I possess a Fast Car.

It is a BMW.

```
>>> azure_sky('supercar', 'Ferrari')
```

I possess a Supercar.

It is a Ferrari.

Everything else in the defined function remained the same except the order of arguments, which ruined everything in the displayed result. So you need to be very careful about the order of the positional arguments. As evident from the name, the position of each argument is very important in these kinds of functions. Now let's move on to adding more than two positional arguments.

```
>>> def azure_sky(car_name, car_type, car_price):

        """Display information about supercars and average cars."""

        print("\nI possess a " + car_name.title() + ".")

        print("It is a " + car_type + ".")

        print("Its current value is " + car_price + ".")



>>> azure_sky('bmw', 'fast car', 'five million dollars')
```

I possess a Bmw.

It is a fast car.

Its current value is five million dollars.

If you have noticed, I have used the title case for car_name while I defined the function, and the output is not so charming. Thankfully, we can change that. Let's do that.

```
>>> def azure_sky(car_name, car_type, car_price):

        """Display information about supercars and average cars."""

        print("\nI possess a " + car_name.upper() + ".")

        print("It is a " + car_type + ".")

        print("Its current value is " + car_price + ".")



>>> azure_sky('bmw', 'fast car', 'five million dollars')
```

I possess a BMW.

It is a fast car.

Its current value is five million dollars.

You can also use lower case to keep the alphabets if needed. Let's see how to do that.

```
>>> def azure_sky(car_name, car_type, car_price):
        """Display information about supercars and average cars."""

        print("\nI possess a " + car_name.lower() + ".")

        print("It is a " + car_type + ".")

        print("Its current value is " + car_price + ".")


>>> azure_sky('bmw', 'fast car', 'five million dollars')
```

I possess a bmw.

It is a fast car.

Its current value is five million dollars.

It is important to remember that when you have written all the *print* codes, you will press the enter button, but the prompt will not show. This happens because the prompt reads the enter as a command to give you an opportunity to enter another code for an additional parameter. This happens if you are using Python 2.5.1. Don't worry. I am also using the same. Just press the enter button once more and you will be able to see the shell prompt right away. One important thing we saw in this function is that we wrote the function just once, but called it multiple times with different positional arguments. We have entered lots of car names and car types as positional arguments in that function, and it efficiently ran each argument. This saved a lot of time that would otherwise have been consumed on defining each function separately to store the value.

Keyword Arguments

We have seen how changing the order of the argument can ruin the function. For longer arguments, chances are higher that you will commit a mistake. But you can get away with that by using the key arguments when you pass information to the function in the form of positional arguments. Let's see how to do that. I'll be using the same function that I have already defined. Once again to remind you, I am using Python 2 shell prompt to write programs. You can download it from www.python.org. Also, make sure to select the right operating system that you have on your personal computer. Versions are different for Linux, Windows and Mac. Let's move on to write the program.

```
>>> def azure_sky(car_name, car_type, car_price):

        """Display information about supercars and average cars."""

        print("\nI possess a " + car_name.title() + ".")

        print("It is a " + car_type + ".")

        print("Its current value is " + car_price + ".")


>>> azure_sky(car_name='bmw', car_type='luxury car', car_price='ten million dollars')
```

I possess a Bmw.

It is a luxury car.

Its current value is ten million dollars.

With the keyword arguments, you can shuffle the order at will or by mistake. It works the same no matter where you have placed the arguments. Let's see try it out.

```
>>> def azure_sky(car_name, car_type, car_price):

        """Display information about supercars and average cars."""
```

```
print("\nI possess a " + car_name.title() + ".")

print("It is a " + car_type + ".")

print("Its current value is " + car_price + ".")
```

```
>>> azure_sky(car_type='luxury car', car_name='bmw', car_price='ten
million dollars')
```

I possess a Bmw.

It is a luxury car.

Its current value is ten million dollars.

The order was changed, but the display remained the same. This method seems to be a bit time consuming but is efficient and fast because there are fewer chances of making a mistake and then getting back to the start to check where you went wrong.

A Look at Argumentative Errors in Functions

Errors are normal when you are programming Python. Sometimes you misplace a comma or misread a whitespace, while at other times you leave a parenthesis empty to trigger a syntax error. Let's see how to deal with them.

```
>>> def azure_sky(car_name, car_type, car_price):

    """Display information about supercars and average cars."""

    print("\nI possess a " + car_name.title() + ".")

    print("It is a " + car_type + ".")

    print("Its current value is " + car_price + ".")


>>> azure_sky()
```

Traceback (most recent call last):

 File "<pyshell#201>", line 1, in <module>

  azure_sky()

TypeError: azure_sky() takes exactly 3 arguments (0 given)

The last line shows that there should be exactly three positional arguments to enter inside the parenthesis. You miss them, and you will have this error in the shell. Let's put two of the arguments and miss one.

```
>>> def azure_sky(car_name, car_type, car_price):

        """Display information about supercars and average cars."""

        print("\nI possess a " + car_name.title() + ".")

        print("It is a " + car_type + ".")

        print("Its current value is " + car_price + ".")


>>> azure_sky(car_type='luxury car', car_price='ten million doallars')
```

Traceback (most recent call last):

 File "<pyshell#204>", line 1, in <module>

  azure_sky(car_type='luxury car', car_price='ten million doallars')

TypeError: azure_sky() takes exactly 3 non-keyword arguments (0 given)

It shows error because you didn't complete the arguments section. A good thing about Python is that it explains where you made mistake that allows you to rectify it right away. Let's analyze the error. The first line tells us to look back to the problem to detect the error in the syntax. It also prints out the call where there is an error. It also tells us how many arguments are missing from the function call.

What we understand from this is that Python reads the code well and tells us how to rectify it. In a blink of an eye, it scans the entire code and returns the error message. (Matthes, 2016)

Python Arrays

Python arrays are used for storing multiple values. Let's see how to do that.

```
>>> carnames = ["BMW", "Ferrari", "Lamborghini", "Bentley"]
```

```
>>> print(carnames)
```

```
['BMW', 'Ferrari', 'Lamborghini', 'Bentley']
```

Array is a special variable that is used to hold multiple values at the same time. Instead of storing different values in separate variables, we use array to cram them in a single variable for ease of use. Array makes it easier for programmers to loop through the cars and track down the value they need. This turns out to be very helpful if you have a thousand values instead of the these four. You can access them individually by using a single line of code. All you need is to remember the index number that a particular value has been assigned. Let's try to access the elements of an array with the help of index numbers.

```
>>> print(carnames)
```

```
['BMW', 'Ferrari', 'Lamborghini', 'Bentley']
```

```
>>> x = carnames[3]
```

```
>>> print(x)
```

```
Bentley
```

```
>>> x = carnames[2]
```

```
>>> print(x)
```

Lamborghini

```
>>> x = carnames[1]
```

```
>>> print(x)
```

Ferrari

```
>>> x = carnames[0]
```

```
>>> print(x)
```

BMW

```
>>>
```

It is easy to access all elements of an array if you remember the index number. As I have already told you, the index always starts at zero.

Modifying the Elements of an Array

You can modify certain elements in the array. If you want a value to be replaced with the new one, you can do that by a single code line if you know its index number.

```
>>> carnames = ["BMW", "Ferrari", "Lamborghini", "Bentley"]
```

```
>>> print(carnames)
```

['BMW', 'Ferrari', 'Lamborghini', 'Bentley']

```
>>> carnames[3] = "Mercedes Benz"
```

```
>>> print(carnames)
```

['BMW', 'Ferrari', 'Lamborghini', 'Mercedes Benz']

```
>>> carnames[2] = "Honda"
```

```
>>> print(carnames)
```

['BMW', 'Ferrari', 'Honda', 'Mercedes Benz']

```
>>> carnames[0] = "Prius"

>>> print(carnames)

['Prius', 'Ferrari', 'Honda', 'Mercedes Benz']
```

Length of an Array

In addition to modification, you can check the length of the array by a single code line. Let's do that.

```
>>> print(carnames)

['Prius', 'Ferrari', 'Honda', 'Mercedes Benz']

>>> x = len(carnames)

>>> print(x)

4
```

Loop the Elements of an Array

You can create loop in array by the following method.

```
>>> carnames = ["BMW", "Ferrari", "Lamborghini", "Bentley"]


>>> for x in carnames:

        print(x)


BMW

Ferrari

Lamborghini
```

Bentley

Other miscellaneous functions of arrays include addition of different elements into the array. All those elements are appended at the end of the array. You can add as many elements as you like. This option allows programmers to keep adding new elements to existing arrays whenever need arises. Let's see the syntax through a real example.

>>> carnames = ["BMW", "Ferrari", "Lamborghini", "Bentley"]

>>> carnames.append("Honda")

>>> carnames.append("Toyota")

>>> carnames.append("Rolls Royce Phantom")

>>> print(carnames)

['BMW', 'Ferrari', 'Lamborghini', 'Bentley', 'Honda', 'Toyota', 'Rolls Royce Phantom']

Also, you can remove certain elements from the arrays. We will have to use the pop method to do so. Let's see how to do that.

>>> print(carnames)

['BMW', 'Ferrari', 'Lamborghini', 'Bentley', 'Honda', 'Toyota', 'Rolls Royce Phantom']

>>> carnames.pop(0)

'BMW'

>>> print(carnames)

['Ferrari', 'Lamborghini', 'Bentley', 'Honda', 'Toyota', 'Rolls Royce Phantom']

>>> carnames.pop(3)

'Honda'

>>> print(carnames)

['Ferrari', 'Lamborghini', 'Bentley', 'Toyota', 'Rolls Royce Phantom']

```
>>> carnames.pop(2)
```

'Bentley'

```
>>> print(carnames)
```

['Ferrari', 'Lamborghini', 'Toyota', 'Rolls Royce Phantom']

```
>>> carnames.pop(4)
```

Traceback (most recent call last):

 File "<pyshell#251>", line 1, in <module>

  carnames.pop(4)

IndexError: pop index out of range

```
>>> carnames.pop(3)
```

'Rolls Royce Phantom'

```
>>> print(carnames)
```

['Ferrari', 'Lamborghini', 'Toyota']

You might have noticed an error message in this snippet of code. I got this message because I tried to pop out the fifth element in the array when it had only four elements. If we go on like that, the array will be empty. Let's continue.

```
>>> print(carnames)
```

['Ferrari', 'Lamborghini', 'Toyota']

```
>>> carnames.pop(2)
```

'Toyota'

```
>>> carnames.pop(1)
```

'Lamborghini'

```
>>> carnames.pop(0)
```

'Ferrari'

```
>>> print(carnames)
```

[]

There is another method for deleting elements from arrays. We have to use the keyword 'remove' to try out this method. A major difference between the pop method and the remove method is that we have to enter the name of the element for the remove method instead of the index number.

```
>>> carnames = ["BMW", "Ferrari", "Lamborghini", "Bentley"]
```

```
>>> carnames.remove("Ferrari")
```

```
>>> print(carnames)
```

['BMW', 'Lamborghini', 'Bentley']

```
>>> carnames.remove("BMW")
```

```
>>> print(carnames)
```

['Lamborghini', 'Bentley']

```
>>> carnames.remove("Bentley")
```

```
>>> print(carnames)
```

['Lamborghini']

(Python Arrays, n.d)

Chapter 9: Python Classes

Just like Java, Python surrounds around objects. Everything in this language is considered an object that has respective properties and methods. A Python class is considered as constructor of objects or a blueprint for creation of objects. Let's see the syntax for creating the class.

```
>>> class AzureSky:

        x = 100


>>> print(AzureSky)

_main_.AzureSky

>>>
```

I have named my class as AzureSky. You can use any name you'd like. It is better to carve out a name in connection with the type of program you are about to write. Classes basically represent real time objects, as well as situations. On the basis of these classes, you are able to create moving objects. In the class, programmers define the characteristics of a particular character and its general behavior.

Python objects, when created with the help of classes, are generally equipped with general behavior. Afterwards, you can allocate unique traits to these objects. This is how you can create real-life situations with the help of Python classes. The entire process of creation of objects is dubbed as *instantiation*. You have to work with instances of classes and hence the name *instantiation*. This chapter will allow you to create classes and then create instances afterwards of those classes. You will learn how to specify the type of information that can be stored in instances. Also, you will define actions that you can take with the help of the instances you have created.

You can store a class in modules and also use other classes that are created by a different programmer in your own programs. This is real-life programming. You will be able to create your own code. You will know your own code and the situations you will create behind it. All you need to understand is the logic behind creation of Python classes. With the help of Python classes, you will be able to make things easier for yourself and other programmers as you will be able to meet up different challenges.

Let's see how to create an object with the help of Python classes.

>>> class AzureSky:

```
x = 100

p1 = AzureSky()

print(p1.x)
```

100

Here I have created the object p1 with the help of the class AzureSky, and then I have printed the value of x.

With the help of classes, you can do remarkable things. I'll create a class that represents a pet cat. You can attribute the character traits that most pet cats usually have. For example, you can assign her a particular name and age. In addition, you can assign her the attribute of sitting and rolling over. We are now giving our cat class four attributes. The first two are static like the name and age while the other two are dynamic like the sitting and rolling features. The cat class will give instructions to Python on how to create an object that would represent a cat.

>>> class Cat():

```
"""I am modelling a Pet Cat"""

def __init__(self, name, age):
```

```
                """"the following are name and age attributes given to
the cat"""

                self.name = name

                self.age = age

                def sit(self):

                        """Stimulate a cat sitting in response to a
command"""

                        print(self.name.title() + " is sitting at the
moment.")

                        def roll_over(self):

                        """Stimulate a cat rolling over when the
command is issued."""

                        print(self.name.title() + " is rolling over
on the ground!")
```

You can notice lots of things here. First of all, you need to see the structure of the cat class. I have defined the class first. Classes are distinct in a way that you have to use capital letters for them. I left the parenthesis empty because this is a newly created class. Once a class is created, the parenthesis can be used to fill different values to accomplish certain tasks.

The statement that is enclosed in triple quotation marks is known as the docstring. It describes what this class is created for.

The third line of the class is the most important of all as it introduces you to a special method, called the *init* method. Let's see what it actually does.

The ___inti___() Method

If we use the *init* method out of a class, it will be safely called a function because that's what it is, by default. But as it is being used in a class, it is dubbed as a method. It is just a change of name as their job remains the same. The init method is special in the sense that Python runs it automatically when a new instance in the cat class is created. You will have to add two underscores in the start and two at the end to help prevent the default method names of Python from conflicting with one another. In the cat class that we have created, the init method has three parameters defined. All three are named as self, name, and age.

Self parameter: this parameter is needed in method. You must put it before the other parameters. This is required by Python, so don't miss it. This is a part of the definition of the *init* method. Every method call that is linked to a class passes the *self* argument. Upon making an instance of cat, Python will refer to the __init__() method that we have defined in the cat class. You will be able to pass the name and age as arguments of the pet cat you are about to create. The *self* parameter passes automatically. Now that everything has been streamlined, we will allocate values to the defined parameters that are name and age, whenever there is a need to create an instance. Just fill in the two parameters with the name and age, and all is done.

When I defined the variables, I attached with them the prefix *self*. Please remember that any variable that you have prefixed with self is connected to all the methods available in a class. You can access these variables with the help of any instance that is created from the class. These kinds of variables are named as *attributes*.

Also, we have added two other methods to the cat class. These are sit() and roll_over() methods, which I have defined. These methods don't require any name or age parameters, so there is only one *self* parameter. Later on, when I will create different instances that will directly access these methods as well, in addition to accessing the name and age parameters. Upon directly accessing these methods, the screen will print that the cat is rolling over or sitting down. That's how instances help us animate the objects that we create.

If you are planning to create a game, you can extend the same concept of the cat class to some more realistic situations. A simple game can allow the users to command the cat to sit and roll over like real objects.

Creating an Instance from the Cat Class

A class is considered as a set of instructions to create an instance. Our cat class allows us to create individual cats with different names and ages. Let's create an instance.

```
>>> class Cat():
        """I am modelling a Pet Cat"""
        def _init_(self, name, age):
                """the following are name and age attributes given to
the cat"""
                self.name = name
                self.age = age
```

```
>>> class Cat():
        """I am modelling a Pet Cat"""
        def _init_(self, name, age):
                """the following are name and age attributes given to
the cat"""
                self.name = name
                self.age = age
                def sit(self):
                        """Stimulate a cat sitting in response to a
command"""
```

print(self.name.title() + " is sitting at the moment.")

def roll_over(self):

"""Stimulate a cat rolling over when the command is issued."""

print(self.name.title() + " is rolling over on the ground!")

#Creating an instance in the cat class.

\>\>\> my_cat = Cat('Tom', 8)

\>\>\> print("The name of my cat is " + my_cat.name.title() + ".")

The name of my cat is Tom.

\>\>\> print("Tom, my pet cat, " + str(my_cat.age) + " years old.")

Tom, my pet cat, 8 years old.

I have successfully created an instance for cat class. I instructed Python to create a cat who is named Tom and is 8 years old. When I entered the information, Python referred back to the __init__ () method in the cat class. The arguments I gave to Python for reference are Tom and 8. The __inti__() method directly created an instance that represented a particular cat and also allocated her a specific name, as well as age. All this information is stored in the instance my_cat. You should take into consideration the nuance between different names. The naming convention is important in a sense that it is easier to remember. The name Cat denotes the cat class while the name my_cat denotes a specific instance you we have just created for the class. That's how it goes on. Otherwise, it gets pretty confusing because in complex games and programs, there are so many classes and instances that it muddled up the mind of the programmer.

You can access individual attributes from the cat class. For this purpose you will have to use the dot notation. Let's access a particular value from the instance that we have just created in the cat class.

```
>>> my_cat = Cat('Tom', 8)
>>> print("The name of my cat is " + my_cat.name.title() + ".")
The name of my cat is Tom.
>>> print("Tom, my pet cat, " + str(my_cat.age) + " years old.")
Tom, my pet cat, 8 years old.
>>> my_cat.name
'Tom'
>>> my_cat.age
8
>>>
```

When we enter an attribute, Python starts working to find out its value in the class, and after that returns the value in a matter of seconds. I attempted to retrieve the values of the name and age of the object I have just created through an instance in the cat class.

How to Call the Methods

When you are done with creating an instance from the cat class, you can use dot notation for calling any method that you have already created in the class. Dot notation is to be used in the same way as you have used for accessing certain attributed from the instances you have created in the class. I have already created a couple of methods for my pet cat. I will be writing the entire class below to refresh your memory about the methods that I have created earlier on. After that I'll show you how to call those methods. Let's roll on.

```
>>> class Cat():
        """I am modelling a Pet Cat"""
```

```python
    def __init__(self, name, age):
        """the following are name and age attributes given to
the cat"""
        self.name = name
        self.age = age
    def sit(self):
        """Stimulate a cat sitting in response to a command"""
        print(self.name.title() + " is sitting at the moment.")
    def roll_over(self):
        """Stimulate a cat rolling over when the command is
issued."""
        print(self.name.title() + " rolled over on the ground!")
```

```
>>> my_cat = Cat('Tom', 8)
>>> my_cat.sit()
Tom is sitting at the moment.
>>> my_cat.roll_over()
Tom rolled over on the ground!
```

I have written the name of the class instance, then I inserted a dot in between and afterwards I wrote the name of the method that I have created in the Cat class. It ran as it was supposed to run. We have successfully created an object named Tom which did what we asked it to do. In this case, Tom sits on the ground when we ask it to. Then it starts rolling over on the ground when it is directed. Just imagine the game in which a cat sits and rolls over on the ground on your instructions. Isn't it amazing?

Just remember the syntax for accessing attributes and calling methods. That's who you can bring objects to life through Python.

Let's move on to creating multiple instances in a single cat class. You can add as many cats in the class as you want to. Imagine a game in which there are four different cats. Let's go on to create the instances for all the four cats.

```python
>>> class Cat():
        """I am modelling a Pet Cat"""
        def _init_(self, name, age):
                """the following are name and age attributes given to
the cat"""
                self.name = name
                self.age = age
        def sit(self):
                """Stimulate a cat sitting in response to a command"""
                print(self.name.title() + " is sitting at the moment.")
        def roll_over(self):
                """Stimulate a cat rolling over when the command is
issued."""
                print(self.name.title() + " rolled over on the ground!")


>>> my_cat = Cat('Tom', 8)
>>> your_cat = Cat('Jerry', 5)
>>> amy_cat = Cat('Tobby', 3)
>>> nanny_cat = Cat('Suri', 2)
>>> print("The name of my cat is " + my_cat.name.title() + ".")
```

The name of my cat is Tom.

>>> print("My cat is " + str(my_cat.age) + " years old.")

My cat is 8 years old.

>>> my_cat.sit()

Tom is sitting at the moment.

>>> my_cat.roll_over()

Tom rolled over on the ground!

>>> print("The name of my cat is " + your_cat.name.title() + ".")

The name of my cat is Jerry.

>>> print("My cat is " + str(your_cat.age) + " years old.")

My cat is 5 years old.

>>> your_cat.sit()

Jerry is sitting at the moment.

>>> your_cat.roll_over()

Jerry rolled over on the ground!

>>> print("The name of my cat is " + amy_cat.name.title() + ".")

The name of my cat is Tobby.

>>> print("My cat is " + str(amy_cat.age) + " years old.")

My cat is 3 years old.

>>> amy_cat.sit()

Tobby is sitting at the moment.

>>> amy_cat.roll_over()

Tobby rolled over on the ground!

>>> print("The name of my cat is " + nanny_cat.name.title() + ".")

The name of my cat is Suri.

```
>>> print("My cat is " + str(nanny_cat.age) + " years old.")
```

My cat is 2 years old.

```
>>> nanny_cat.sit()
```

Suri is sitting at the moment.

```
>>> nanny_cat.roll_over()
```

Suri rolled over on the ground!

I created four cats named Tom, Jerry, Tobby, and Suri. Python was instructed to tell the audience their names and ages and involve them into two actions of sitting and rolling over. That's how you can create as many instances in a single class as you want to. For example, there is a game in which players have to hunt down birds by shooting them with a gun. You can create as many birds as you want your player to shoot down. The methods can be different. Your bird will be flying instead of sitting and rolling over. And after a successful flight it will fall on the ground when your player will shoot them down.

You can create another class for learning purposes. Let's do that.

```
>>> class Restaurant():
        """I am modelling a Restaurant"""
        def _init_(self, restaurant_name, dinner_type):
            """the following are name and type attributes given to
the restaurant"""
            self.restaurant_name = name
            self.dinner_type = dtype
        def describe_restaurant(self):
            """Describe the restaurant as per the informmation"""
```

print(self.name.title() + " is a fast food restaurant.")

def open_restaurant(self):

"""Shows that the restaurant is open."""

print(self.name.title() + " is open from 8pm to 12 am."

How to Work with Classes and Instances in Python

Let's delve deeper into the world of classes. You can use them to simulate some real-life situations. I hope by now you have understood that all you need is to write the class first. After that you can insert as many instances in the class as you need. Now, once you have created an instance, you can modify its attributes either directly or by writing a method that will eventually update the attribute in particular ways.

Let's once again to the cat class that I have created for you, and apply certain methods to the class for greater variety and flexibility in programming.

>>> class Car():

"""I will represent a car by this class"""

def _init_(self, make, model, year):

"""The following attributes will describe a car"""

self.make = make

self.model = model

self.year = year

def get_descriptive_name(self):

"""I will return a well-formatted descriptive name."""

```
            long_name = str(self.year) + ' ' + self.make + ' ' +
self.model

            return long_name.title()
```

```
>>> my_car = Car('BMW', 'az', 2005)

>>> print(my_car.get_descriptive_name())

2005 Bmw Az

>>> your_car = Car('Ferrari', 'B3', 2009)

>>> print(your_car.get_descriptive_name())

2009 Ferrari B3

>>> amy_car = Car('Mercedes Benz', 'B3', 2009)

>>> print(amy_car.get_descriptive_name())

2009 Mercedes Benz B3

>>> nanny_car = Car('Lamborghini', 'B3', 2009)

>>> print(nanny_car.get_descriptive_name())

2009 Lamborghini B3

>>>
```

I defined the __init__ () method with the help of self parameter. I entered three parameters that were to be used later on in the class. I stored all the three in attributed and afterwards used all the three in the class instances I created later on. As a whole, I created four instances. You can add more to the list. For each newly created instance, I had to specify the attributes of make, model, and year of a particular car. That's how I moved on with creation of instances.

After that, I defined a method for each instances, which in this case is get_descriptive-name(). This method prints the name, the model and the year of manufacturing of a particular car. You can use this type of class and instances on your website to show the customers to navigate through to know more about the products that are available in the store. They can see the models, names, and make of all the cars. In this way, you can make your web application more interactive. This method allows us to cram all values in a single string and print it right away. If you don't use this function, you will have to assign all attributes the same values by picking them one by one.

Assign Default Value to an Attribute

We can assign default values to an attribute. Now I'll add an attribute named odometer_reading to the same car class. It will show us the mileage of the car. For this attribute we'll have to add a new method called read_odometer() to the class that will show readings of the odometer of a particular car. Let's do that.

```
>>> class Car():
        """I will represent a car by this class"""
        def __init__(self, make, model, year):
                """The following attributes will describe a car"""
                self.make = make
                self.model = model
                self.year = year
                self.odometer_reading = 0


        def get_descriptive_name(self):
                """I will return a well-formatted descriptive name."""
                long_name = str(self.year) + ' ' + self.make + ' ' +
self.model
```

```
        return long_name.title()

    def read_odometer(self):

        """It will print a statement that will tell about the
mileage of a car."""

        print("Your car shows " + str(self.odometer_reading) +
" miles on the meter.")
```

```
>>> my_car = Car('BMW', 'az', 2005)

>>> print(my_car.get_descriptive_name())

2005 Bmw Az

>>> my_car.read_odometer()

Your car shows 0 miles on the meter.
```

We have successfully added a new method to the code and also run it to get the desired value. As we know, mileage of a car tends to change more often and that we will have to change the value. Do we need to write the entire coding right from point A? Well, I don't think so. We can modify an attribute's value. Let's see how to do that. I will display the entire code for your ease of learning. Let's see how it is done.

```
>>> class Car():

    """I will represent a car by this class"""

    def _init_(self, make, model, year):

        """The following attributes will describe a car"""

        self.make = make

        self.model = model

        self.year = year
```

```
            self.odometer_reading = 0


    def get_descriptive_name(self):
        """I will return a well-formatted descriptive name."""
        long_name = str(self.year) + ' ' + self.make + ' ' +
self.model
        return long_name.title()
    def read_odometer(self):
        """It will print a statement that will tell about the
mileage of a car."""
        print("Your car shows " + str(self.odometer_reading) +
" miles on the meter.")


>>> my_car = Car('BMW', 'az', 2005)
>>> print(my_car.get_descriptive_name())
2005 Bmw Az
>>> my_car.read_odometer()
Your car shows 0 miles on the meter.
>>> my_car.odometer_reading = 35
>>> my_car.read_odometer()
Your car shows 35 miles on the meter.
```

Also, you can change it as many times as you want to, and for as many cars as you need to. Let's see how to do that for four different cars.

```
>>> class Car():
```

```python
"""I will represent a car by this class"""
def __init__(self, make, model, year):
        """The following attributes will describe a car"""
        self.make = make
        self.model = model
        self.year = year
        self.odometer_reading = 0


def get_descriptive_name(self):
        """I will return a well-formatted descriptive name."""
        long_name = str(self.year) + ' ' + self.make + ' ' +
self.model
        return long_name.title()
def read_odometer(self):
        """It will print a statement that will tell about the
mileage of a car."""
        print("Your car shows " + str(self.odometer_reading) +
" miles on the meter.")


>>> my_car = Car('BMW', 'az', 2005)
>>> print(my_car.get_descriptive_name())
2005 Bmw Az
>>> my_car.odometer_reading = 35
>>> my_car.read_odometer()
Your car shows 35 miles on the meter.
```

```
>>> my_car = Car('Ferrari', 'b7', 2008)

>>> print(my_car.get_descriptive_name())

2008 Ferrari B7

>>> my_car.odometer_reading = 25

>>> my_car.read_odometer()

Your car shows 25 miles on the meter.

>>> my_car = Car('Ferrari', 'b7', 2008)

>>> print(my_car.get_descriptive_name())

2008 Ferrari B7

>>> my_car.odometer_reading = 35

>>> my_car.read_odometer()

Your car shows 35 miles on the meter.

>>> my_car = Car('Lamborghini', 'u7', 2002)

>>> print(my_car.get_descriptive_name())

2002 Lamborghini U7

>>> my_car.odometer_reading = 55

>>> my_car.read_odometer()

Your car shows 55 miles on the meter.

>>>
```

(Matthes, 2016)

How to Modify the Value of an Attribute by a Dedicated Method

You can also update the value of a particular attribute with the help of a dedicated method. The method you will use will simply pass on the new value to the attribute and displays it right away. This is easier than the other method. You can change the value frequently with this method. Let's see an example that shows how to add a method and update the value of the attribute that returns the mileage of a particular car. Let's code.

```python
>>> class Car():
        """I will represent a car by this class"""
        def __init__(self, make, model, year):
            """The following attributes will describe a car"""
            self.make = make
            self.model = model
            self.year = year
            self.odometer_reading = 0


        def get_descriptive_name(self):
            """I will return a well-formatted descriptive name."""
            long_name = str(self.year) + ' ' + self.make + ' ' +
self.model
            return long_name.title()
        def read_odometer(self):
            """It will print a statement that will tell about the
mileage of a car."""
            print("Your car shows " + str(self.odometer_reading) +
" miles on the meter.")
        def update_odometer(self, mileage):
```

        """This will set the reading of the odometer to the given value."""

        self.odometer_reading = mileage

```
>>> my_car = Car('Lamborghini', 'u7', 2002)
>>> print(my_car.get_descriptive_name())
2002 Lamborghini U7
2002 Lamborghini U7
>>> my_car.read_odometer()
Your car shows 0 miles on the meter.
>>> my_car.update_odometer(55)
>>> my_car.read_odometer()
Your car shows 55 miles on the meter.
>>> my_car.update_odometer(33)
>>> my_car.read_odometer()
Your car shows 33 miles on the meter.
>>> my_car.update_odometer(45)
>>> my_car.read_odometer()
Your car shows 45 miles on the meter.
>>>
```

I created a class and instances. After that, I simply changed the value of the mileage through this method. There is no need to change anything in the class or in the instance. This is simple, fast and efficient.

We can also get some additional work from this method. You can put a stopper in the code by which no one will be able to roll back the odometer.

```python
>>> class Car():
        """I will represent a car by this class"""
        def __init__(self, make, model, year):
                """The following attributes will describe a car"""
                self.make = make
                self.model = model
                self.year = year
                self.odometer_reading = 20


        def get_descriptive_name(self):
                """I will return a well-formatted descriptive name."""
                long_name = str(self.year) + ' ' + self.make + ' ' +
self.model
                return long_name.title()
        def read_odometer(self):
                """It will print a statement that will tell about the
mileage of a car."""
                print("Your car shows " + str(self.odometer_reading) +
" miles on the meter.")
        def update_odometer(self, mileage):
                """
                This will set the reading of the odometer to the given
value.
```

Thiw will reject any change if any attempt is made to roll back the odometer.

```
        """

        if mileage >= self.odometer_reading:

                self.odometer_reading = mileage

        else:

                print("Sorry, you don't have the permission to
roll back the odometer!")
```

(Matthes, 2016)

Another method allows you to increment a value that has been assigned to an attribute. For example, our car changes its value as time passes. We can keep a record of the addition by a simple method. It will increment its value without tinkering with the entire class. Let's see the syntax and the result in a real class.

```
>>> class Car():

    """I will represent a car by this class"""

    def __init__(self, make, model, year):

            """The following attributes will describe a car"""

            self.make = make

            self.model = model

            self.year = year

            self.odometer_reading = 20


    def get_descriptive_name(self):

            """I will return a well-formatted descriptive name."""
```

```python
        long_name = str(self.year) + ' ' + self.make + ' ' +
self.model

        return long_name.title()

    def read_odometer(self):

        """It will print a statement that will tell about the
mileage of a car."""

        print("Your car shows " + str(self.odometer_reading) +
" miles on the meter.")

    def read_odometer(self):

        """It will print a statement that will tell about the
mileage of a car."""

        print("Your car shows " + str(self.odometer_reading) +
" miles on the meter.")

    def increment_odometer(self, miles):

        """This will add more amount to the odometer reading
as given by the user."""

        self.odometer_reading += miles


>>> my_car = Car('BMW', 'b5', 2005)

>>> print(my_car.get_descriptive_name())

2005 Bmw B5

>>> my_car.increment_odometer(100)

>>> my_car.read_odometer()

Your car shows 120 miles on the meter.

>>> my_car.increment_odometer(5500)

>>> my_car.read_odometer()
```

Your car shows 5620 miles on the meter.

>>> my_car.increment_odometer(1000)

>>> my_car.read_odometer()

Your car shows 6620 miles on the meter.

>>> my_car.increment_odometer(5000)

>>> my_car.read_odometer()

Your car shows 11620 miles on the meter.

>>>

It takes the existing number of miles and adds the new value into it, and displays the result afterwards. That's how as your car gets aged, you can keep incrementing the value. That's how you can create a program in which a user can enter his or her mileage values. But you need to install proper security checks in order to bar users from accessing the areas where you have defined the methods.

Child Class and Parent Class

We can create a class within a class by the child class method. Let's create an ElectricCar class within the parent class. This child class will be able to use all the attributes of the parent class. You can also write a specific code just for the child class. As for its placement, it comes right after haven written the parent class. Let's do that.

>>> class Car():

    """I will represent a car by this class"""

    def __init__(self, make, model, year):

        """The following attributes will describe a car"""

        self.make = make

        self.model = model

```python
        self.year = year
        self.odometer_reading = 20


    def get_descriptive_name(self):
        """I will return a well-formatted descriptive name."""
        long_name = str(self.year) + ' ' + self.make + ' ' +
self.model
        return long_name.title()


    def read_odometer(self):
        """It will print a statement that will tell about the
mileage of a car."""
        print("Your car shows " + str(self.odometer_reading) +
" miles on the meter.")


    def update_odometer(self, mileage):
        if mileage >= self.odometer_reading:
            self.odometer_reading = mileage
        else:
            print("Sorry, you don't have the permission to
roll back the odometer!")


    def increment_odometer(self, miles):
        """This will add more amount to the odometer reading
as given by the user."""
```

```
                self.odometer_reading += miles


>>> class ElectricCar(Car):

        """This will carry details on supercars only."""

        def __init__(self, make, model, year):

                """This will intialize attributes that I have given to the
parent class."""

                super().__init__(make, model, year)

(Matthes, 2016)
```

Chapter 10: File Navigation with Python

You can make your programs more relevant and usable if you know about file navigation in Python. This chapter will show you how to manage files in Python. You can use files in the midst of programs to quickly analyse bundles of data.

Python offers several functions from creation of files to updating, reading and removal of files. All this in a very easy way.

Reading Information from a File

Files can hold a diverse number of data. One of the types is a text file that can store a literary research paper, information on the weather changes, and graphs on the socioeconomic condition of a particular country. With the help of Python, you can read a complete file and also rewrite it in the form that a browser finds it easier to display. Let's see how you can work with a text file. The first step of working on a text file is of course reading it. First of all, create a file txt file with the following contents in it.

3.1415926535
8979323846
2643383279

Store this file in the same directory where you are saving Python programs. Then enter the following in the Python sell to ask Python to read the file that you had saved and then display its contents right away.

```
>>> with open('digits..txt') as file_object:

        contents = file_object.read()

        print(contents)
```

The first line in this program has a duty to open the function. It accesses the relevant file that you want to be displayed. There is just one argument involved in the open function and that is name of the file that you want to access. When you enter the function, Python starts its search in the directory where the Python program that you are executing is stored. If you don't store it in the same directory in which your Python program is stored, you will be unable to display the contents as Python will totally miss it.

Let's create a text file in Python. The step 1 to do that is as under:

f= open("testfile.txt","w+")

The W in this code represents the word write. The adjacent plus sign indicates that the code will create a file that doesn't exist in the syst em. Let's move now towards step 2 of the code. We will be using a fo r loop for the second step. The loop will run through 20 numbers. T hen I will use the write function for filling data in the file. I will ente r a piece of text that will be iterated in the file. In the same line of te xt, we will be the percent d which is a display integer. Now it is time to close the file.

```
>>> def main():
    # This will create a file in the system which is will be in the text form
at.
        f= open("testfile.txt"."w+")
    # I will enter some data into the text file.
        for i in range (20):
            f.write("I am creating a file %d\r\n" % (i+1))
    # Now it is time to close the file.
        f.close()
```

Let's see some code snippets to navigate through files. For reading a file the following code is required to be filled in the Python shell.

f = open("testfile.txt", "r")

print(f.read())

Also, you can choose which part of the file you want to read. The following method used for purpose.

f = open("testfile.txt", "r")

print(f.read(5))

(Python File Open, n.d)

Pattern Matching

With the help of module regular expressions, we can specify a set of strings(pattern) that ultimately matches it. In order to fully underst and this, we need to go through the MetaCharacters. There are fourt een of them. A RedEx or is usually a sequence of characters that will ultimately form a search pattern. RegEx are used by programmers t o locate certain search patterns in a string.

Let's take a look at the RegEx Module. Fast forward to Python shell. Let's try it out.

```
>>> import re
>>> #This is to check if the strig is going to start with "Rain" and ends
with ""Heaven":
>>> txt = "Rain is falling down from the heavens"
>>> x = re.search("^Rain.*heavens$", txt)
>>> if(x):
          print("Yes, There is a match!")
```

```
Yes, There is a match!
>>>
```
Let's take a look at RegEx functions. This helps us find the matching patterns in Python strings. Time to demonstrate.

```
>>> import re
>>> #This is to check if the strig is going to start with "Rain" and ends
with ""Heaven":
```

```
>>> str = "Rain is falling down from the heavens"
>>> x = re.findall("in", str)
>>> print(x)
['in', 'in']
>>>
```
You might be thinking what happens if there is no match found by t he Python shell. Let's see.
```
>>> import re
>>> #This is to check if the string has got the word angels:
>>> str = "Rain is falling down from the heavens"
>>> x = re.findall("angels", str)
>>> print (x)
[]
>>> if(x):
        print("Yes, we have found angels in the string.")
    else:
        print("Sorry, we have not match.")
```

Instead of using if statement, you can simply print the string and see whether there is a match or not.
```
>>> import re
>>> str = "Rain is falling down from the heavens."
>>> x = re.search("angels", str)
>>> print(x)
None
>>>
```

Now, I'll introduce you to the search function in pattern matching.

```
>>> import re
>>> str = "Rain is falling down from the heavens."
>>> x = re.search("\s", str)
>>> print("We have out first white-space character located in position: ", x.start())
('We have out first white-space character located in position:', 4)
>>>
```

You also can split up the string into separate words with a simple function. Let's see how to do that.

```
>>> import re
>>> # I am going to split up the string at each white-space character.
>>> str = "Rain is falling down from the heavens."
>>> x = re.split("\s", str)
>>> print(x)
['Rain', 'is', 'falling', 'down', 'from', 'the', 'heavens.']
>>>
```

An amazing thing about this function is that you can demonstrate greater control over it. You can decide which white-space you would like to split up your string. Here is the syntax to achieve this purpose.

```
>>> import re
>>> # I am going to split up the string at each white-space character.
>>> str = "Rain is falling down from the heavens."
>>> x = re.split("\s", str, 2)
>>> print(x)
['Rain', 'is', 'falling down from the heavens.']
>>>
```

Python not only allows you to match different patterns, it also permits substitution in the strings. Let's see how it is done.

```
>>> import re
>>> # I am going to substitute all white-space characters with a single digit 5.
>>> str = "Rain is falling down from the heavens."
>>> x = re.sub("\s", "5" , str)
>>> print(x)
Rain5is5falling5down5from5the5heavens.
>>>
```

When you are substituting something in the string, you can limit the number of substitutions in the string by a simple function. For exa mple, you can restrict the number of substitutions to 2 in the string. This is how you can have greater control over your functions.

```
>>> import re
>>> # I am going to split up the string at each white-space character.
>>> str = "Rain is falling down from the heavens."
>>> x = re.sub("\s", "5" , str, 2)
>>> print(x)
Rain5is5falling down from the heavens.
>>>
```
(Python RegEx, n.d)

Exploring the Match Object
You can search for a match in the string and then move on to some really interesting things. First of all, run the function that shows a match. I know you have already done that, why not do it just one more time? Also, this time it is different.

```
>>> import re
>>> # I am going to split up the string at each white-space character.
>>> str = "Rain is falling down from the heavens."
>>> x = re.search("in", str)
>>> print(x) # this should print an object.
<_sre.SRE_Match object at 0x025BF218>
>>> print(x)
<_sre.SRE_Match object at 0x025BF218>
>>> print(x)
<_sre.SRE_Match object at 0x025BF218>
>>>
```

The Match subject has certain properties and methods that can be used to retrieve information about the search as well as the result. Let's see how to do that.
.span()   This one tends to return a tuple that contains the start-, and in addition, the end positions your match.

.string()   This one tends to return the string that has been passed into the function
.group()   This one tends to return the part of the string where it finds a match.

Now we shall move on to examples.

```
>>> import re
>>> # I am going to search for the upper case "R" character in the start
 of a word.
>>> str = "Rain is falling down from the heavens."
>>> x = re.search(r"\bR\w+", str)
>>> print(x.span())
(0, 4)
```

The following function will print the string that is passed on to the function.
```
>>> import re
>>> # The property of the string will return the search string.
>>> str = "Rain is falling down from the heavens."
>>> x = re.search(r"\bR\w+", str)
>>> print(x.string)
Rain is falling down from the heavens.
>>>
```

The following function will search for any words that starts with the word R and then prints it out.

```
>>> import re
>>> # I am going to search for the upper case "R" character in the start
 of a word.
>>> str = "Rain is falling down from the heavens."
>>> x = re.search(r"\bR\w+", str)
>>> print(x.group())
Rain
>>>
```

Conclusion

Python is one of the most used programming languages across the world. The wide range of application of Python is a combination of some key features that attract programmers. Let's take a look at some of the benefits of Python.

- The Python Package Index(PyPI) has multiple 3rd party modules. On the back of these, Python has become capable of interacting with lots of other programming languages. This has made Python really attractive to programmers. As each day passes, more and more programmers are learning Python.

- Open source is another attraction of Python. It is free to use and is even distributed for commercial reasons. The Python community collaborates for development of Python code, mailing lists, and modules, which makes Python an extremely rich language.

- Unlike other programming languages, Python is considerably easy to learn. It is very readable. You can take a look at the code and understand most of it even if you have never done computer programming in your life. The syntax is simple for beginners to understand.

- Then comes the support libraries, which include string operations, Graphical User Interfaces (GUIs) for Operating Systems, etc. You will be able to find lots of high-profile programming task in Python libraries. They are already scripted and available for use. This you will save the effort you need for writing the code.

The benefits of Python are great. Without a doubt, this is why Python is one of the most popular languages across the world today.

Its syntax is made to allow programmers to write clean code. You will see that the code will be perfectly human-readable. In addition, you will be able to remove any bug in the blink of an eye in case you end up having an error. Take the following as an example:

```
>>> myset = {"BMW", "Ferrari", "Mercedes Benz", "Toyota", "Lamborghini", "Rolls Royce", "Baleno", "Prius", "Tesla Land Rover"}
```

```
>>> myset = {"BMW", "Ferrari", "Mercedes Benz", "Toyota", "Lamborghini", "Rolls Royce", "Prius", "Tesla Land Rover"}
```

```
>>> myset.remove("Baleno")
```

```
Traceback (most recent call last):
  File "<pyshell#35>", line 1, in <module>
    myset.remove("Baleno")
KeyError: 'Baleno'
```

You can clearly see that Python tells us where the problem lies. It also shows which word has a bug. You can directly reach the core of the error and remove the bug right away. This makes Python easy and speedy at the same time.

Python can be used to create games and develop web apps. Businesses hire Python experts to solve problems related to their network systems or software related issues. You can also use Python for scientific research because of its unique automation features.

In addition, the Python community is incredible. It is so vast and so generous that you'll always feel at home. Experienced programmers are always ready to offer their advice while beginners are ready to learn and share the problems they are facing. Their problems are well catered by the masters of Python. When the solution is paired up with the problem, we have a marvelous package of problem-solving for learners. You can get your problems solved just by reading previous posts left by fellow programmers. This is how learners and masters keep contributing to the Python community, which sets it apart from other programming languages.

I'd like to wish you the best of luck in your ongoing programming journey and would like to remind you to be on the lookout for the next book in this series which will give you a deeper look under the hood on Python. Meanwhile, check out my other books on the applications of Python from data analytics to machine learning.

Thank you for reading this book and best of luck!

Resources

Hetland, Magnus Lie, (2008). Beginning Python
From Novice to Professional,
Second Edition, [PDF File]

Matthes, Eric, (2016). PYTHON
CR ASH COURSE. [PDF File]

Python Dictionaries. Retrieved from
[https://www.w3schools.com/python/python_dictionaries.asp]

Python Data Types. Retrieved from
[https://www.w3schools.com/python/python_datatypes.asp]

Python File Open, n.d. Retrieved from
[https://www.w3schools.com/python/python_file_open.asp]

Python Sets. Retrieved from
[https://www.w3schools.com/python/python_sets.asp]

Python if...else, n.d. Retrieved from
[https://www.w3schools.com/python/python_conditions.asp]

Python Arrays, n.d. Retrieved from
[https://www.w3schools.com/python/python_arrays.asp]

Python RegEx, n.d. Retrieved from
[https://www.w3schools.com/python/python_regex.asp]

Python Functions, n.d. Retrieved from
[https://www.w3schools.com/python/python_functions.asp]

www.ingramcontent.com/pod-product-compliance
Lightning Source LLC
Chambersburg PA
CBHW071126050326
40690CB00008B/1355